real
coaching
and feedback

11

018

Books that make you better

Books that make you better. That make you *be* better, *do* better, *feel* better. Whether you want to upgrade your personal skills or change your job, whether you want to improve your managerial style, become a more powerful communicator, or be stimulated and inspired as you work.

Prentice Hall Business is leading the field with a new breed of skills, careers and development books. Books that are a cut above the mainstream – in topic, content and delivery – with an edge and verve that will make you better, with less effort.

Books that are as sharp and smart as you are.

Prentice Hall Business.
We work harder – so you don't have to.

For more details on products, and to contact us, visit
www.business-minds.com
www.yourmomentum.com

■ *real* skills for *real* results ■

real
coaching and
feedback

how to help people improve
their performance

JK SMART

Prentice
Hall

BUSINESS

An imprint of **Pearson Education**

London • New York • Toronto • Sydney • Tokyo • Singapore • Hong Kong • Cape Town
New Delhi • Madrid • Paris • Amsterdam • Munich • Milan • Stockholm

PEARSON EDUCATION LIMITED

Head Office:
Edinburgh Gate
Harlow CM20 2JE
Tel: +44 (0)1279 623623
Fax: +44 (0)1279 431059

London Office:
128 Long Acre
London WC2E 9AN
Tel: +44 (0)20 7447 2000
Fax: +44 (0)20 7447 2170
Websites: www.business-minds.com
          www.yourmomentum.com

First published in Great Britain in 2003

© Pearson Education Limited 2003

The right of JK Smart to be identified as author of this work has been asserted
by her in accordance with the Copyright, Designs and Patents Act 1988.

ISBN 0 273 66328 3

British Library Cataloguing in Publication Data
A CIP catalogue record for this book can be obtained from the British Library

10 9 8 7 6 5 4 3 2 1

Designed by Claire Brodmann Book Designs, Lichfield, Staffs
Typeset by Northern Phototypesetting Co. Ltd, Bolton
Printed and bound in Great Britain by Bell & Bain Ltd, Glasgow

The publishers' policy is to use paper manufactured from sustainable forests.

To Sandy, who lifts my spirit
and nurtures my soul.

With thanks to Darren Hayes
and Savage Garden for providing
the soundtrack to the writing.

Contents

PART 2
Getting coaching right in the *real* world 53

Appendices 145

About the author

Karen Smart's background is in individual and organizational development. However, unlike some in her field, first and foremost Karen sees herself as a line manager. In recent years, she's worked primarily on enabling managers to manage – developing and delivering everything from individual skill building and management development programmes to management systems design and organization wide culture change. In addition to managing her team, Karen has coached senior managers and facilitated cross-functional working, problem solving and conflict management. Although she has two degrees and has researched extensively across a range of disciplines, ultimately Karen feels she's learned most about management from her experience as an overworked and undervalued manager, disempowered by bureaucracy. From this experience – and inspired by the man she says 'puts the J into JK Smart and a lot of the smart too' – the philosophy of *real* management for *real* people was born.

■ *real* management for the way it is ■

Introduction to *real* management

▶ **Welcome to the *real* world**

Do you read most management books and say, 'If only it was that easy in the real world'? *Real* management is the answer for every manager who knows it's about doing the best we can with what we've got, in the real world of organizations that are demanding more and more for less and less. It's for real managers who think the books we've read must have been written by people who don't live in our world and who mistake us for superheroes. We know we could work out a better way of managing if only we could get off the treadmill long enough to find the time.

▶ **Telling it like it is**

But what if someone had read everything, tried everything, worked out why things don't work in the real world, found a way of managing that works with the complexity of real life instead of pretending it's simple, and then taken time off from managing to tell you about it? And what if that someone wasn't a guru, academic or consultant but an ordinary, overworked manager who knows what managers are up against and who doesn't judge or preach or try to

1

get people to be something they're not? And what if that same manager understood that the idea of 'one size fits all' doesn't work and offered you a way of blending her insight with your experience so you could become the manager you were meant to be?

Real management:

- Makes sense of your experience by explaining why, when we do things by the book, they don't work.

- Is based on a common-sense understanding of human nature that takes your concerns seriously and starts from the assumption that what you're doing now makes sense for the situation you're in.

- Helps you turn your past experience into the key that unlocks your best ever management performance.

1

Confessions of an overworked manager

Towards a new way of managing in the *real* world

I'm tired of being overworked – are you?

I'm not a management guru. I'm an overworked manager who got sick of being overworked. I love my work so I give it 100 per cent . . . I push my team . . . we achieve things . . . I'm given more work . . . I give it 110 per cent . . . I push my team a bit harder . . . we achieve more things . . . I'm given more work . . . need I go on? Stress researchers say our automatic response to overload is to do what we were doing before only harder and for longer. Psychologists say insanity is doing the same things over and over and expecting different results. So, as they say in America, 'You do the math!'

There has to be a better way of working

Psychologists also say that if you want a different result, you have to do something different. Since I started my management career, I've seen (and been guilty of) the sorry way managers treat their staff (and vice versa), and I've become increasingly disillusioned with the established wisdom about managing people. I began to believe there had to be a better way.

> **Beliefs** are thoughts we use to guide our decisions and actions, although we tend to forget and see them as indisputable facts. With any action, a belief always comes first. We find evidence to support our beliefs in our experience. Once we've got a belief, we tend not to question it, unless an experience forces us to.

People shouldn't have to leave their brains at the door or become robots when they come into work. They shouldn't have to run ever harder just to stand still. In recent years, I've watched people go sick with stress and I've seen stress-management programmes being offered as the cure, all the time thinking that we must be in big trouble if we're settling for *managing* stress instead of removing it at source. I knew there had to be a way to remove the stress caused by the gap between who we are outside of work and who we have to be at work. There had to be a way of managing that isn't soul-destroying for everyone involved. I just didn't know what that way was. Then I met someone who changed the way I think about people; who motivated me to find a new way of managing; who influenced me to want to be a better manager; and who inspired me to take time out and write this series of books in the hope that I could do for others what he did for me.

There had to be a way of managing that isn't soul-destroying for everyone involved.

Getting out of the box of traditional management thinking

I started as a management trainee on a year's development programme, during which I became fascinated by the way people manage, and I've been a student of management as well as a manager ever since. I'm exaggerating (but, sadly, only slightly) when I say that by the time I decided there had to be a better way, I'd already read and tried everything ever published about management. Clearly, if I wanted new answers I had to look in new places. Not one to do things by halves, I've looked close to management, in neuroscience, psychology and psychotherapy to learn how our brains work, why we do the things we do, and how to deal with emotions and the effects of early conditioning on our behaviour. And I've looked far from management – everything from aikido to Zen Buddhism via horticulture and homoeopathy (well, if we aren't growing something as managers, we're curing it, right?). And yes, I confess, I've read almost everything the self-help movement has to offer, sifting the sensible from the senseless.

Looking for what makes sense

After years of being a task-focused manager working for organizations in 'initiative' mode, I can assure you I'm too sceptical about the 'next new idea' and the 'one size fits all' solution to have bought into any one set of beliefs. Instead, what I've done is collect and use the ideas that made sense of my experience. Small sentence, big idea, so let me say it again. I researched a wide range of subjects and whenever I got a feeling of 'that's obvious', I applied the idea to the way I manage and used my experience to figure out what worked.

> **Trial and error** is how we learn from experience – trying to do something, noticing what doesn't work, and changing our approach until we find what works. More often than not, we decide what works and doesn't work based on the feedback we get.

I want to make it easier for you than it was for me

It would be hypocritical for me to tell you I'm sceptical of people who sell you the 'one right way' and then try to do the same thing myself, so that's not what I'm doing. I'm sharing what I've learned to save you having to do all the research I did. But I can't do it all for you – we have to be in it together.

Equal partners or no deal

Ninety-five per cent of what we learn comes from experience, with only five per cent coming from books, training, etc., and they only work when they resonate with our own experience by triggering memories of earlier experiences.

> We have vast quantities of experience that we can't hold in our **conscious minds** so we store these experiences in our sub-conscious. The trouble with our **subconscious** is that it's sub (below) conscious (the level of our awareness) so we aren't conscious of (don't know) what's in there. We need triggers to surface it.

A good book is, in effect, telling you something you already know intuitively; you just haven't articulated it on a conscious level.

Intuition is that feeling of knowing something, without knowing how you know it. It means you're using information from your subconscious mind that your conscious mind isn't aware of.

What I'm telling you will work only if you use my insight as a trigger for surfacing your experience and intuitive (subconscious) insight because, in the end, only your insight can improve your performance. It's 'equal partnership learning' – I provide the trigger, you provide the experience. I have no ambition to create clones of me. I want people to manage in a way that works for them – a way that suits their unique blend of insight and experience. What I *am* hoping for, though, is that you'll think what I'm saying is common sense.

Common sense (a rarity in life) is when something is both logical (appealing to our conscious minds) and intuitive (appealing to our subconscious minds) and we get a 'that's obvious' feeling. When our conscious and subconscious minds are out of sync, we get an 'off' feeling – something isn't quite right, but we don't know why.

So, as you read this book, think about your experience and see if you get a 'that's obvious' feeling. If you do, then try my approach, learn from it, and adapt it to meet your needs. If you get an 'off' feeling, then challenge what I'm saying, come to your own insight, try that, learn from it, and adapt it to meet your needs.

Starting from where people are

The biggest mistake people make when trying to help move someone forward is to assume they're both starting from the same place – something that never happens in real life. I don't want to make that mistake with you, so throughout this book – in shaded boxes – I explain the concepts and beliefs that underpin my approach to management. In Appendix 1, there's also a broader look at where I'm coming from as a manager.

Let's keep it real here

If you're like most managers I know, you won't have time to read a heavyweight volume (even if I had time to write one), but you won't want to be fobbed off with one-minute answers that only work in books either. So what I've done (to give you the best of both worlds) is to put some powerful messages – that hopefully will resonate with your own experience and trigger your insight – into a quick but intense read. There's also a reminder of the key messages and some questions to think about at the end of each chapter.

Let me know what you think

I mean what I say about being equal partners, so if you want to share your experience and insight or ask questions about anything in the book, I'd really like to hear from you. You can email me at **JKSmartBooks@aol.com**. I take on a few telephone coaching clients each year so managers who are interested may email me as may trainers and development specialists who are interested in attending an 'equal partners learning programme' to be licensed to work with this material.

IN SHORT

▶ We can't keep doing what we've always been doing because it doesn't work and it stresses us out in the process.

▶ People who still tout the established management wisdom are 'flat earthers' who need to be challenged to develop an approach that works in the real world.

▶ I'm not telling you anything you don't already know: I'm only helping you to bring your insight to the surface where you can do something with it.

▶ Challenge everything I say, and take away only what makes sense of your experience.

2

The key to unlocking your best ever performance

Track back from your experience, then work forward from your beliefs

We already have everything we need to be effective

We just have preferences for, and are more skilled in, some things than others (a result of them being our preferences). Development, especially in people skills, isn't about teaching new skills as much as about unblocking existing ones. What blocks our development? Our beliefs, which govern how we use our characteristics. Lack of self-belief is the single biggest block to excellent performance. Once you get that sorted, everything else falls into place.

But our beliefs hinder us from using them

You may have excellent communication skills, but if you believe that talking never solved anything, then they're not likely to get much of an outing, so how will you ever know just how good they are? Have you ever thought, 'I wish I could do that but I'm not confident/bright/calm/etc. enough'? What are the component parts of the skill you wish you had? Do you use them in any other activity or part of your life?

And so do our judgements about ourselves

What's your biggest strength? Okay, in what kinds of situations does it really help you to perform well? Now identify at least one situation in which it hinders your performance. You may find this hard, but persevere, because I guarantee there will be at least one. If in doubt, ask a trusted colleague. Now, relabel the strength as a neutral word or phrase that would apply equally to both the helpful and hindering situations. When you've done that, try the same exercise again but this time for your biggest weakness and, suddenly, we don't have strengths and weaknesses any more; we have characteristics.

A **characteristic** is a piece of knowledge, an attitude, a behaviour, a skill, or any single input you bring to your performance. It is described neutrally to avoid implying strength or weakness. For example, I'm not lazy, I'm someone who doesn't like to waste energy. The same characteristic can be helpful or hindering depending on the context in which it is used.

The need to find and challenge our hindering beliefs

Are you happy with your results in all areas of your life? People are happy with their performance when the external world matches their inner reality and unhappy when it doesn't.

My definition of **sanity** is when the external world matches the picture of it that we have in our minds without us having to distort either what's out there or what's in our minds. It's when we see things as they are, not as we wish they were.

There are people who are happy or unhappy for healthy reasons (they see things as they really are and not as they'd like them to be). There are also people who are happy (but delusional) or unhappy (but victims) for unhealthy reasons (they distort what they see to conform to their inner reality).

Our **subconscious creates experiences** for us (from events) that reinforce what we believe about the world and the people in it, if necessary by distorting the picture so we see only what we want to see. But, while it does this to keep us feeling sane on a day-to-day basis (yes, even when all around us think we're delusional), it craftily creates negative experiences when it wants to push us into re-examining our beliefs. And if we don't re-examine our beliefs after a negative experience, it keeps recreating the same experience until we give in and do what it wants.

Effectiveness is when people are happy for healthy reasons. If you're not happy with the responses you're getting and the experiences you're creating, then you have three choices:

1. Carry on as you are, a victim in your own melodrama, blaming circumstances or other people and dragging the rest of us down with you.

2. Reframe the results so that you turn them into a positive experience that you can be happy about.

> **Reframing** is when we change our interpretation of an event, usually by challenging the beliefs that underpin our original interpretation. We do this by finding other ways of looking at it.

3. Assume what you got was what you wanted and track back to the beliefs that drove the behaviour. If you're okay with the beliefs, then go back to option 2. If you're not, then re-examine them and develop alternatives to change your behaviour and achieve different results.

We all know how to do option 1 but what about the rest? Easier said than done? Yes, if you associate change with behaviour change, but I'm talking about belief changes that take milliseconds to achieve and last forever and – and this is the big plus – a changed belief triggers a changed behaviour in ways that don't require mountains of will-power to sustain. Want to give it a try? Read on . . .

A changed belief triggers a changed behaviour without requiring mountains of willpower.

IN SHORT

▶ You've got everything you need already; it's only your beliefs that are holding you back.

▶ Stop being so hard on yourself: being judgemental and self-critical never helped anyone improve.

▶ Take the acid test: ask yourself if you're happy with the results that you are achieving.

▶ If you're not happy, don't just sit there; do something about it.

3

If it's as easy as the books make out, why are there so many books?

Resisting the temptation to want easy answers in a complex world

It's not my fault – it's the way I'm programmed

It's scientific fact, mother! Wanting easy answers doesn't make me lazy. Brains are hard-wired to lay down programmes in our subconscious so we can do things without thinking (on autopilot, if you like), leaving us with plenty of spare capacity to deal with the unexpected.

The brain develops **programmes** in our subconscious, based on our experiences. When it registers an unfamiliar event, it quickly (so quickly we don't know it's happening) looks for a suitable pre-existing programme (**pre-programme** for short) to interpret the event (like a computer matching fingerprints). When it registers a good enough match, it automatically triggers the response from the earlier experience.

Trainers call the pre-programmes that serve us well 'unconscious competence'.

> At the bottom of the learning ladder is **unconscious incompetence** (when we don't know what we don't know), then **conscious incompetence** (when we realize we need to learn something), followed by **conscious competence** (when we're mastering a skill and still have to concentrate all the time we're doing it). This stage continues until we can do it without having to think (**unconscious competence**). Driving is the classic example.

So many choices – so little time

The trouble with being an overworked manager is that the only time I get a taste of the huge variety today's world has to offer is when I'm skimming the Sunday papers, and let's face it, who has time to do more than skim when there's so many sections? I used to like that line in Kipling's *If* about filling the unforgiving minute with 60 seconds' worth of distance run . . . until I had to live it! Ignoring the fact that some of today's time-saving devices don't actually do what they say on the tin (I'd mention email, but don't get me started on that or we'll be here all day), it's the ever increasing expectations of what we're meant to do with the time we save that get me. It's as though if we're not working flat out to improve the quality of our relationships, bodies, spirits and lifestyles – and don't forget careers – then we're somehow failing to make the most of everything that twenty-first-century life has to offer.

Is it any surprise that, as managers, we want one-minute answers to twenty-year problems? Who has time to spend with their staff these days, when the pressure to deliver more outputs with fewer resources is greater than ever? No wonder hypocrisy creeps in, as on a recent appraisal training course, where a group of management-level appraisees had no problem saying that for their own appraisal they wanted their manager to take as much time as it needed to do a good job, but that they were far too busy to do that for their team members.

The customer is king – so give them what they want

An IT manager asked me to approve a plan for recruiting IT officers for a number of local offices around the country. He wanted to run the selection process at HQ, with IT experts interviewing and then allocating successful candidates to local managers. He wanted the recruits to have high-quality IT skills, and he knew local managers weren't IT literate enough to ensure that. Something wasn't right with his proposal (my 'off' feeling), so I probed and discovered he feared local managers wouldn't have ownership of the national IT strategy if they'd had no say in the appointment of their IT officer. In the end, we recruited at local level with an IT person doing the shortlist (for quality control) and asking the technical questions, but with the local line manager making the final decision. The solution gave the IT manager everything he needed, which he wouldn't have got if I'd just given him what he wanted.

A lot of organizations buy into the 'customer is king' myth, and so must many management writers, otherwise quick-fix, autopilot, 'one-size-fits-all' solutions wouldn't be so prevalent on the management shelves of your local bookstore. Books that offer solutions that would insult your intelligence if you weren't so distracted by the demands of your job. Solutions that *do* insult your subconscious intelligence if only you had time to listen to it. And when you *do* look beyond the glib answers, what do you find? A complex world overcomplicated by impenetrable academics or the fashionable world of the latest management guru who thinks you can solve everything by applying an alarmingly alliterative acronym!

We need *real* answers for the way it is in the *real* world

Real managers run a mile from formulaic approaches that treat human beings as a constant when they're a variable. We know people make money by giving us what we want regardless of whether it's what we need, but in the *real* world what's important is what works, not what's quick. We need to find a way to meet our conscious need for easy answers with our subconscious need for a common-sense approach that works with the complexity of human nature.

IN SHORT

▶ We may be programmed to want easy answers, but we don't have to give in to temptation.

▶ We have so many choices about how to spend our time that it makes sense not to waste time getting our people management wrong.

▶ What we want isn't always what we need, so we need to think before we buy what's on offer.

▶ Yes, we *want* easy answers, but we *need* answers that work, so let's not settle for shabby compromise: let's get the best of both worlds.

PART 1

■ *real* management for the way it is ■

Understanding why coaching and feedback goes wrong so you can put it right

▶ Understanding the cause and effect relationships

As an overworked manager, I find it easy to get sucked into dealing with problems at symptom level rather than root cause. I get a buzz out of taking decisive action so I find it hard to slow down and make the effort to understand why something has gone wrong, even though I know the buzz won't last any longer than my solution.

▶ Taking a long hard look at the way we coach

If you're anything like me, you'll be itching to get straight to the 'how to do it' part. But remember, that's where we went wrong in the past, so please bear with me because we can't put something right unless we understand why it went wrong in the first place. In a quick read, I don't have time to give you lots of examples plus my insights, so I'm going to explore one big example in depth. I've used a composite of several real-life experiences, so I can highlight the issues that undermine our approach to coaching.

4

Why can't I just send them on a training course?

Coaching reaches the parts that training cannot reach

Meet Jenny, the bane of my life

Jenny was a trainer, an excellent one, on a team I once managed. She had a way with people that made them feel comfortable, and her facilitation skills were always complimented by course participants. I've never seen her angry, or even mildly annoyed for that matter. She was softly spoken and liked long periods of reflection before she came to a decision (you can tell I've moved on, as at the time I wouldn't have used a neutral characteristic – I'd have just called her indecisive). Everyone liked her . . . except for me (which made me feel quite the bad guy, I can tell you). I thought she was a wimp (now that *is* an honest reflection of my position at the time). Maybe that's why I tended to notice the things she couldn't do more than the things she could do.

Outside the training room, her performance was inconsistent. She got her messages across brilliantly in the training room and was a lively communicator, but put her in a meeting and she became tentative and confusing when she did speak, which wasn't often. She wrote excellent handouts and training materials, but her reports were a mess. And, for a woman with a master's degree, she could be really stupid. I can't abide people who waste their talent and, though she did a good job as a trainer, she was capable of doing so much more if only she would get her act together.

If training is the answer, what's the question?

I thought about coaching her – after all, I did it with other team members – but, to be brutally honest, I didn't relish the prospect of working that closely with her. But she had things that needed to be sorted out so I thought I'd start small – with her report writing. She had an important report to write over the next two months so it would be a timely training intervention.

(As I write this, I finally realize that a big part of my problem with Jenny was my projecting on to her a characteristic I'd denied in myself – my wimpish streak. I mean if sending her on a training course instead of coaching her myself isn't a wimpish act, what is?)

We're **projecting** when we see in others some 'thing' (a thought, belief, characteristic or whatever) that we have in ourselves but don't see and wouldn't like if we did (which is why we don't). Our subconscious wants us to be mentally healthy, which means accepting every part of us, so it keeps showing us the bits we deny by projecting them on to other people – the ones who push our buttons. That person usually has the 'thing' in a small way, enough of a hook to hang our projection on, but not enough to justify our reaction. One of the

> best ways of knowing that you're projecting is when the person
> who pushes your buttons doesn't do it with others. That's when
> you know your reaction is telling you more about you than the
> person you're reacting to.

Feeling guilty for copping out, I chose the best and most expensive report-writing course I could find. It ate up far more than her share of my training budget, and it took her out of the office for three whole days, which was a real drag, but it would be worth it.

Jenny came back from the course having thoroughly enjoyed it and saying she'd learned a lot, so I decided to let her loose on the big report. The report was to give proposals for an empowerment strategy. Jenny had worked for months with various groups of stakeholders to develop proposals, which included a massive training programme that would cascade from top to bottom of the organization. When I saw her first draft a couple of weeks later, I had to face facts – it was no better than her previous reports. Training hadn't been the answer to Jenny's problems. But then, why would it be? I hadn't been looking for the answer to Jenny's problem, had I? I'd been looking for the answer to my problem about not wanting to coach her.

The development buck stops with the manager

Oh dear! I'd only fallen into the same bad practice I criticized other managers for. I'd sent Jenny on a course and expected her to come back 'cured', and I'd tried to shift my management responsibility for her development on to some poor hapless trainer who knew nothing about her performance in the job so was handicapped before they even started. It was embarrassing to admit this to myself, so I wasn't going to admit it to anyone else – I'm a manager whose specialism is individual and organizational development, for goodness' sake! I'm supposed to know better! And I do, which is, perhaps, the worst admission of all.

You can do it – training can help

Do you remember that old advert: 'You can do it, we can help, one calorie, one calorie, Diet Pepsi can help'? But do you remember the bottom of the screen, where it said, in very small print, 'Only as part of a calorie-controlled diet'? That reminds me of training. Training – at least, good-quality, focused training that really involves the participant – can help but only as part of a controlled development process. On a training course, the trainer's aim is to guide participants around the learning cycle, so they:

- Tend to begin by offering some kind of insight. A good trainer will go beyond the theoretical knowledge by sharing their own insight (what they've learned from their experience of applying it). A bad trainer (and sometimes these are the very people who think they're good because they believe they can train in any subject regardless of whether they can 'do' the skill) will, like a bad actor, just deliver their lines.

- Follow up with a discussion or an activity designed to help participants challenge their existing insight and, hopefully, question any hindering beliefs or bad habits that might be undermining their performance.

- Give an opportunity, through exercises or role plays, for participants to practise what they've learned.

- Aim for the course to become an 'experience' in its own right.

> **Experience = event + interpretation**
> Very little of what we call our experience is made up of things that happen to us (events). Most of it is about how we interpret (make sense of) those events.

- Ask the participant to review their experience of the course and learn from it, either at the end of the course or afterwards.

Sounds great in theory, but in practice it's not the ideal learning experience because:

- people tend to be spoon-fed someone else's insight instead of being encouraged to arrive at their own, so what they've learned doesn't stick because it doesn't integrate with the rest of their experience and insight;

- many trainers can't handle being challenged, and it's difficult for people to learn from someone else's insight if they aren't able to challenge that insight;

- Role plays may be fun (if you like that kind of thing – which I don't), but stop and think about exactly what we're learning. We're learning how to do something in a 'safe' environment ... which is about as helpful as exam results are in telling you anything except how good people are at taking exams. Work isn't a safe environment ... especially when the other person hasn't been on the same course so doesn't play by the same rules.

Work isn't a safe environment ... especially when the other person hasn't been on the same course so doesn't play by the same rules.

If formal training is to become improved job performance (and why else are we doing it?), then it has to be one step in a bigger process – which is where coaching comes in.

A word for my fellow control freaks

Have you known people to come back from a course wanting to do things differently and you've put them off because you don't know what they've learned and you're wary of allowing uncontrolled changes? With coaching, you're in control of what people learn and how they apply it, so you can make sure it fits their operating context.

> **Operating context** includes anything or anyone in your organizational or external environment that affects performance. Primarily, that means people (customers, suppliers, colleagues, staff and stakeholders), your organizational culture and the external factors affecting your organization.

If I can do it, I can coach it – right?

If I say so myself, I know a thing or two about report writing – so I could manage to coach Jenny, right?

The best player doesn't necessarily make the best coach – and vice versa

I reckon that, whatever the field (and I include management in this), there are maybe three types of expertise out there:

1. *Instinctive players,* who are competent but don't know how they do it. These include the real geniuses, the ones whose performance just flows, but it also includes many of us who've been doing our work for so many years that we can do it in our sleep. We're what trainers call unconsciously competent. People who are unconsciously competent often don't make good coaches because they can't analyze their performance so they don't know what makes it competent. And, especially for those with the genius touch, it's probably just as well, because if they tried, they'd probably find their 'game' dropped off.

2. *Analytical players*, who are competent and can analyze what they're doing and explain it to someone else. If I could analyze my performance (find a way to shift from unconscious competence back to conscious competence), I could at least tell Jenny what competent performance consisted of. It wouldn't be coaching, but it would be a step in the right direction.

3. *Coaching players*, whose play is okay but who are never going to make the top flight (usually they're missing a vital component of performance). However, they can watch someone else play and tell you what's wrong with their 'game'. And, as they can analyze good performance as easily as bad, they can help people shift from one to the other. So, if I was going to be coach, I needed to be able to analyze Jenny's performance as well as my own.

IN SHORT

▶ **Training only works as part of a bigger, coaching process.** Do you ever send people on courses when you know you should be coaching them yourself?

▶ **Coaching and playing are separate skills.** Do you feel confident about being a coach? If not, what can you do about it?

5

Why doesn't my feedback and coaching work?

The myths of 'constructive criticism' and 'one-size-fits-all'

Coaching isn't just about passing on our wisdom

I talked to Jenny and she agreed to be coached, so we had a coaching session in which I gave advice on the best way to write reports for our organization – the kind of insider knowledge she wouldn't get on a training course. I thought the session went quite well (she seemed to be making a lot of notes anyway). I suggested she try applying my advice to her draft report and let me see a second draft.

After all my coaching effort, I was disappointed to find that the second draft wasn't better than the first. It didn't flow.

I sometimes get **flow problems** when I'm reading draft reports, and I have a simple technique for putting things right. I cover up everything except the first paragraph, which I read as if I'm new to the subject. Then I pause and see what questions naturally arise. Then I uncover the next paragraph to see whether it either answers them or gives a cross-reference to the answer. If it doesn't do either, I find the answer and either move it so it follows immediately or add a cross-reference. Then I repeat the process for each paragraph in the rest of the report. Once you get the knack, it doesn't take very long and it can really transform an uninspiring or unpersuasive read.

I said as much to Jenny. I stressed how important it was for us to get the report right: the subject matter was controversial and we really needed to persuade the right people to support our proposals as we weren't going to be able to please everyone so we needed powerful allies. She was very quiet throughout, with a look on her face that made me feel like I'd kicked a lame dog.

Constructive criticism is an oxymoron

I'm cutting a long story short here – I promise you I didn't just hit her with it the way I've described. Obviously, I started and ended on good points about her writing skills in handouts and training material (the good old sandwich technique), but I confess there was no way of disguising the fact that I was criticizing her work.

To be honest, I have no idea why the **sandwich feedback technique** ever caught on, as the **primacy and recency effect** means it defeats its object. This effect describes what happens when we're given a long list of things to memorize. We remember most easily the first (primacy) and last (recency)

> things on the list and tend to forget the bits in the middle, which, in the case of feedback, is the very bit we want to be remembered.

The reality is that by criticizing Jenny, I put her on the defensive (in her own unique, wimpish way), and the defensive is a place where learning can't happen. When I think of some of the so-called constructive criticism I've had, I shouldn't have been surprised at Jenny's defensiveness. Most of the people who've criticized me have seen it as helpful feedback, but it wasn't helpful at all. And calling something feedback doesn't make it feedback – if it's judgemental, it's criticism.

Calling something feedback doesn't make it feedback – if it's judgemental, it's cricitism.

Feedback is about observations, not judgements

I should have treated Jenny like I'd have treated a colleague who'd produced a poor report but who I didn't have 'criticism rights' over. I ask questions to provide a framework for them to critique their own work. Questions like:

- What are we hoping to achieve with this report?
- What are the key questions the people who are reading it will want answers to?
- Does it take people through our line of thought so they can see not just what we want but where we're coming from?

After Jenny had gone, I had a long, hard think about why someone as bright as she was, who could write great handouts and training materials, should write such hopeless reports. Something shifted in me as I was thinking it through, and I could feel myself becoming genuinely curious about Jenny's inconsistent writing skills. Looking back, I reckon that was the shift that saved the day.

I got Jenny back in and explained my curiosity, but the conversation didn't go where I thought it would go. Jenny gave me some feedback on my coaching performance and she did it a lot better than I did.

Learning about the different ways different people learn

She was clever, I must say. She didn't talk directly about my coaching at all. She told me a story about her best ever experience of learning a new skill. It was what people in the training trade would call a 'narrative-rich discussion'.

> **Narrative-rich discussions** are those in which you basically get someone to tell you the whole story of the event. If they give you the little details, the nuances, their feelings (all the story's local colour), you can learn so much more about what's happening than you can with a 'just give me the hard facts' approach.

It turned out that Jenny liked to think things through and come to her own conclusions about how best to try out what she'd learned, and she liked to ask questions to be sure that what she was learning fit with the rest of her thinking. I got the message. My 'tell and sell' approach – the one that worked well with other members of the team – hadn't worked for her.

IN SHORT

- **There's no such thing as constructive criticism.** How do you feel when you are criticized?

- **Feedback is neutral, not judgemental.** Be honest: do you give feedback or judgement (whether criticism and praise)?

- **Everyone learns differently.** Do you know how your team members learn?

6

Why, even when my coaching works, does it not improve performance?

Targeting the right area and taking yourself out of the equation

Solving the wrong problem

Never one to give up until I've tried everything, I decided to suspend judgement about Jenny's weaknesses and start analyzing her performance as a whole. And this time I was going to look for things that didn't add up. It was so obvious, I don't know why I hadn't seen it before. If she could write great handouts and training material, then the problem couldn't lie in her writing skills – it must be some characteristic she used for report writing that she didn't use when writing handouts and training material.

Working *with* instead of *on* Jenny

Jenny and I explored possible explanations for the variations in her performance. She said her writing was good when her thinking was clear, but poor when it was fuzzy. (It was at about that point when I began to wish I'd asked her those questions about the report as I'd have seen her lack of clarity of thinking for myself.)

Getting below the symptoms to the root cause

What Jenny was saying made sense of why she wrote well in some situations and not in others, but it didn't make sense of why she could think well enough to get a master's degree but not to write a report on a subject she knew like the back of her hand. I was getting the hang of this analyzing thing, so I asked Jenny to tell me more about her thinking processes. She described the way she developed training courses in some depth, and it was obvious that by the time she got around to writing the materials and handouts she was really clear about what she wanted to say. In fact, she said the handouts practically wrote themselves. Reports, however, were a different thing altogether, and she felt she never seemed to achieve the same clarity about what she was doing. The big problem seemed to start a lot earlier than the writing stage. It started when she was faced with resolving the differing views of the various stakeholders and coming up with proposals that pleased all of them.

> I divide **stakeholders** into **interest and impact groups**. Impact groups can prevent you achieving the outcomes. Interest groups will be affected by the outcome but can't prevent you achieving the outcomes. You can't ignore the needs of either group, but the distinction helps when you're managing a conflict of interests.

That's when I began to realize that thinking, like writing, was a symptom, and the problem might be to do with managing conflict and confrontation. Jenny confirmed that she didn't like upsetting people. Within her comfort zone of the training room, where any conflict was low-level, she just had more ways of handling it – using pre-programmes she'd developed over many years as a trainer.

And it helped that she was in charge so had 'trainer authority' over the participants. In meetings, on the other hand, she was out of her comfort zone and just part of the team, so her problem with conflict was more exposed.

How I contributed to the problem

I know that two things bear on performance – the characteristics of the performer and the impact of factors beyond their control – but it took some facing to realize that I was a factor affecting Jenny's performance. But there it was, clear as day. My way of running team meetings didn't bring out the best in Jenny. I do my best work when I'm challenged, so there's nothing I like better than a good debate of the issues, and I encourage everyone to speak their minds and challenge each other. But it was all too cut and thrust for Jenny. We were always in each other's face and, although the rest of us wouldn't even have labelled it conflict, to Jenny it felt like a war zone.

Two things bear on performance – the characteristics of the performer and the impact of factors beyond their control.

Deciding on a two-pronged approach

In the light of this new, shared understanding, we agreed that Jenny would work on her skills at managing conflict and I would work on adapting team working so it worked for her as much as for the rest of us. Things were finally beginning to look up.

IN SHORT

▶ **Getting to the root cause of a performance problem is essential.** Have you ever had an experience like mine where you've developed the wrong thing?

▶ **Managers are sometimes a factor affecting performance that reduces team member impact.** If I asked your team members whether you ever hindered their performance, what would they say?

▶ **Work with people, not on them.** Do you treat your team members as equal partners in their development?

7

Why is it such hard work to correct people's weaknesses?

Focusing on weakness instead of building from strength

Trying to make a confronter out of a conciliator

Credit where it's due, Jenny worked hard to become better at confronting issues and managing conflict across the whole spectrum of her job. But there was still something not right. I just couldn't put my finger on what it was – she walked like a confronter, she even talked like a confronter, but she wasn't a confronter.

When we're observing and listening, our conscious picks up the words and the more obvious behaviour and our subconscious picks up the rest. Because our subconscious notices everything and because it's stronger than our conscious, we tend to form our judgements from the way people behave rather than from what they say. Our **subconscious is**

▶

designed to spot inconsistencies, which it tells us about through our intuition. Because all this happens below our level of consciousness, we often just get a feeling that we don't trust someone, but if we analyzed it we'd find we've picked up an inconsistency between their words and deeds.

What was becoming increasingly clear was that the harder Jenny tried to be a confronter, the more stressed she became. As time went by, the stress started to have a knock-on effect on aspects of her performance that usually worked well for her. It was as if in trying to be something she wasn't, she was pulling her whole performance out of sync.

Exploiting strengths to compensate for weaknesses

I remembered the definition of insanity being about doing the same things over and over and expecting different results so I decided to try something different. Jenny's dislike of confrontation must have led her to develop strong facilitative and consensus building skills, so maybe we could use them to compensate.

We worked together to identify ways in which she could reframe situations that she normally judged as confrontational. For example, we built on the way she'd given me negative feedback earlier so she could use it with her staff. We developed ways of managing conflict where, instead of focusing on compromises (I can never say the word 'compromise' without pairing it with the word 'shabby') that pleased no one, she'd use her good brain to generate real synergies that pleased everyone. Jenny tried out the ideas and was happy with the results. It felt easier than direct confrontation, she said, yet she didn't feel she'd compromised on the outcomes.

Working with who people are and not who we'd like them to be

Once I'd stopped expecting Jenny to be a confronter, and started working with her on how to make the most of her strengths, the improvements in her performance just started to flow.

And helping them feel good about themselves

The other thing I noticed was how much more confident Jenny looked. Clearly her success was making her feel good about herself. And the better she felt about herself, the more willing she was to take risks to try new ideas to improve her performance. And the more her performance improved. We were on a roll.

IN SHORT

▶ **Don't try to correct weaknesses: try to outweigh them with strengths.** Have you ever been on the receiving end of someone trying to make you into something you're not?

▶ **Use your thinking skills to find ways of exploiting what people have already got.** What difference would it have made to how you felt if the person trying to make you into something you're not had, instead, valued what you were and worked with that?

8

Why doesn't the performance improvement stick?

Breaking the cause and effect chain of hindering beliefs

When being skilled isn't enough

You're **skilled** when you can consistently produce your desired effect. Some people would argue that if you make someone feel snubbed, for example, you do not have good interpersonal skills. I say that if that's what you intended, then you're skilled and if it's not what you intended, you're not.

For several months, Jenny's performance continued to show improvements, but then I started to notice her slipping back into her old conflict-avoidance ways. By this time, I'd put a lot of work into coaching her so I wasn't about to give up, even if she was. We had a review for learning, and she described her most recent confrontation experience. I learned that she had to stay focused all the time to keep her new approach going.

This was odd. Obviously, that's necessary while someone's in the conscious competence stage of learning but eventually we're supposed to make it to the unconscious competence stage, so it happens naturally. Why wasn't that happening with Jenny? It certainly wasn't lack of practice, which can be one reason for a drop-off in performance.

When new behaviour clashes with old beliefs

As she described the feelings she got when she confronted, she rambled a lot, so I almost missed a reference to not wanting to upset people. Something about the way she said it felt 'off', so I asked why she thought she would upset people and she replied that people didn't like being confronted. I asked how she knew that, and her reply surprised me. She assumed that because she didn't like confrontation (which explained a lot about the problems in my relationship with her), other people didn't like it either. This led to her doing as she would be done by, despite the fact that not everyone's tastes are the same. So, while her conscious mind was pushing her towards a new set of behaviours, her subconscious mind was pulling her back towards her old behaviours because that was what matched her beliefs.

What it boiled down to was this: we had created a way for Jenny to do something she didn't like doing that was easier for her to manage and suited her character, but we had completely failed to address the fact that she still didn't like doing it.

When we ignore the evidence that clashes with the old beliefs

Of course, Jenny was ignoring the fact that many of the people on whom she'd used her new skills had actually thanked her for being straight with them and had shown no signs whatsoever of being harmed by the experience. But then Jenny's subconscious couldn't allow her reticular activating system to notice evidence that didn't support her belief – not when its job is exactly the opposite.

> **Reticular Activating System** (RAS) is a brain function that makes us notice things that are significant to us but not notice things that aren't. We need it because there's so much information to process all the time that without it we couldn't function. But guess which bit of the brain decides what we need and don't need to see? That's right, the subconscious!

When I overrode Jenny's RAS by telling her that there were many people like me (who preferred to know where they stand with other people) who might actually feel more harmed by her avoidance approach than by confrontation, she was plunged into a state of cognitive dissonance.

> **Cognitive dissonance** happens when we try to hold two opposing thoughts at the same time. The mind can't cope with it, so it works hard to get rid of the inconsistency (dissonance) in one of three ways:
> **1.** By reducing the importance of the dissonant beliefs.

2. By increasing the number of consistent beliefs to outweigh the dissonant ones.
3. By reinterpreting the dissonant beliefs so they're no longer inconsistent.

I know a smoker who uses all three!

Jenny had to get her head around the idea that avoiding confrontation was a way of avoiding harm *and* of doing harm at the same time.

Getting Jenny's subconscious on board for the change

As we talked about her beliefs, it came across strongly to me that Jenny placed a lot of value on not causing harm to people, and that she sincerely believed that confrontation was a source of harm. By asking questions to explore where she was coming from, I managed to get her to separate out her value about not harming people from her belief that confrontation harmed. She began to see that what she needed was to find a belief that gave her a better approach to achieving her value.

Moving from 'push' mode to 'pull' mode

I suggested that before she tried more behaviour changes, she spend time observing the people she had regular dealings with and working out what their needs were. I suggested she use her imagination instead of her empathy, as I felt that would give her a more detached approach.

I prefer **imagination** to **empathy** because empathy is so easy to get wrong. Too often, people think empathy is about how we'd feel if we were in someone else's situation. But we get it wrong because we take our own frame of reference with us, whereas if we actually were in their situation, we'd be looking from a different perspective so we'd feel and do things differently. Getting this wrong is often what stops us understanding people.

I asked Jenny not to think about how she would feel if she was the one being confronted but to really observe and listen to how it made them feel. Only when she had a better feel for the effect she was having on people could she start thinking about new ways to use her consensual approach.

IN SHORT

▶ **Our beliefs drive our use of our characteristics.** What hindering beliefs are blocking your performance?

▶ **Challenging our RAS helps us change our beliefs.** Look back to a negative experience and ask yourself what seems obvious now that you didn't see then.

▶ **Getting your subconscious on side makes all the difference.** Identify a change you have made where you had to force yourself to sustain it, and then identify one where you feel it just happened naturally; then ask yourself what was the difference between the two.

9

Why, even when I do everything right, does it still go wrong?

Because we're human beings, not robots – thank goodness

What I learned from my coaching experience

I learned that if I'd been a better coach, I'd have spent more time analyzing Jenny's performance and less time judging it, so I'd have improved our relationship as well as her skills. And if I'd treated her as a person in her own right, I'd have found out what she needed and worked with her strengths, so we'd have made progress more quickly without damaging her self-esteem. And if I'd understood how beliefs influence behaviour, I'd have seen her performance for what it was, an indicator of hindering beliefs, and I would have helped her challenge her thinking, which would have enabled her to improve her own performance.

Asking the tough questions

If we don't get the results we want, we have to face the possibility that we wanted our coaching attempts to fail. If so, we need to accept that no matter how much we know logically (consciously) that we need to coach more, our subconscious wants something else more. And whatever it is, our subconscious will sabotage our efforts until we resolve the discrepancy. If your coaching attempts haven't worked as you would have liked, it may be because you fell into some of the same traps as I did. But before you start changing your approach, it's worth checking to see whether you really do want to coach – by asking yourself . . .

What do I gain when coaching goes wrong?

Do you like people to do things the way you do? Are you better at telling than asking? Do you find it uncomfortable that coaching makes you look at yourself as much as the person you're coaching? I answered yes to all these questions. Making the admission worth the effort means not self-judging but just accepting that human beings are complex and we do the best we can at the time to respond to our needs.

Human beings are complex and we do the best we can at the time to respond to our needs.

Like most things to do with human nature, our **needs** are simultaneously complex and simple. Simple because we have only two core needs – to avoid pain and to get pleasure (or, as we get older and more sophisticated, to avoid negative consequences and to seek positive consequences). Complex because our beliefs about what causes pain and pleasure are unique to us.

It doesn't make us bad people, it just makes us human. But what if we don't use what we've learned to move ourselves forward? Well, maybe that's when we should be giving ourselves a good talking to!

You already know everything you need to produce your best ever performance

Events happen, we interpret them to create an experience, and then we store them in our subconscious. So why aren't we already effective? The reasons may be:

- The way we interpreted the event – which caused us to believe something that isn't realistic. Did we miss some of the lessons by looking at it only in one way?
- We're only working with our conscious mind (our logic) – so we're not listening to our subconscious mind (our intuition). And if we're doing that, we aren't accessing all our experience in making our interpretation.

I use the term 'logic' to mean our unique concept of rational cause and effect. Everyone has their own logic, so if you work backwards from the effects people achieve and ask yourself why someone would want to do that, you will find the belief that caused them to produce that effect – that's their logic.

- We're only working with our subconscious mind – operating on autopilot and not using our conscious mind to check that what we're doing is logical. And if we're doing that, we're acting like children in situations that require us to act like adults.

The only way to be effective is to have your logic and intuition in balance. It's only common sense, after all.

Using this book to trigger your subconscious knowledge and insight

If people learn from experience, what's the point of reading a book? No point at all if you don't make it into an experience. Remember:

Event + interpretation = experience

So if you just read the book, you've had an event, not an experience, and you won't learn anything from it. A good book will do three things:

- It will make you think, interpret and maybe challenge some of your beliefs and, in doing so, will become an 'experience' in its own right.

- It will bring to the surface things you already know on a subconscious level from your experience of life so you can look at them more closely.

- It will expose you to someone else's experience so you can learn from that in the same way that you learn from your own experience and, in doing so, save yourself time and aggravation.

But it won't work if you read it on autopilot

I hope that as you read the rest of the book, you will pause each time something triggers either of the following responses:

- If you want to say, 'Well that's just common sense', stop and ask yourself, 'Am I acting on what I know?' and 'Would other people be able to tell that's what I believe from the way I behave?'

■ If you get an 'off' feeling, stop and work out what's making you feel like that. You don't have to agree with everything I say. My insight is only here to trigger yours – it's what makes sense to you that matters.

If you get an 'off' feeling, stop and work out what's making you feel like that.

IN SHORT

❯ We do what makes sense to us, so suspend self-judgement and look for your logic. What do you have to gain when your coaching attempts go wrong?

❯ If we're not as effective as we'd like to be, then we need to reinterpret our experiences. Looking back to your last experience of coaching, what might a neutral observer say you'd missed?

❯ A good book will trigger things that your subconscious knows already. What has made sense to you so far?

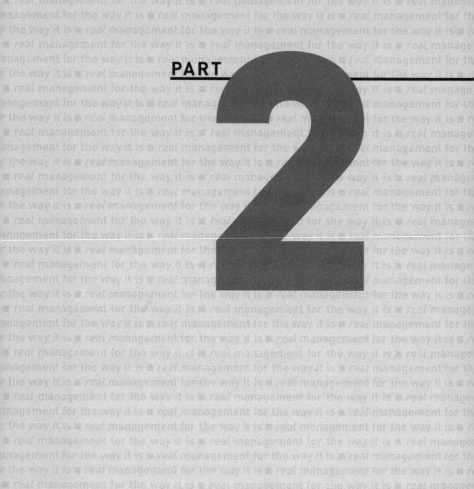

PART 2

■ *real* management for the way it is ■

Getting coaching right in the *real* world

If you're anything like me, you've skipped straight to this page because it explains the coaching process from first thoughts to final review for learning. Never mind telling me why it goes wrong, I hear you mutter, just tell me how to do it right. I wish I could but, sadly:

■ Learning is about trial and error, and the more you can learn from my trials and errors (in Part 1), the less time you need to waste doing your own.

■ When it comes to getting results in the real world, you can't pin your faith on the kind of task-oriented processes that operate in most organizations. Why not? Because human beings have a habit of putting spanners in the works of even the best laid processes.

Process is important, I grant you (there's really no other way to get from start to finish in anything we do), but a process that's been

53

designed without a proper understanding of what *can* go wrong *will* go wrong.

How many times have you felt that you were serving a process that should be there to serve you? On my good days I see process as a necessary evil, but on my bad days it's the enemy that makes me manage like a robot. And speaking of enemies, I like the martial arts idea of deflecting your opponent's strength against itself, so I design inclusive processes that take account of all the things that normal processes leave out, things that make me more people-oriented.

▶ It's not my process that matters – it's yours

Most management writers will tell you to 'follow this process and you'll be fine'. I only wish it was true. But the truth is, no one but you can know what it's like in your world, so no one but you can design a coaching process that works for you. What I can do is describe seven generic steps that will identify all the things you need to think about when you're designing your own coaching process. So, as you read through each step, remember the insights you got from reading Part 1 and think about how you can use the process to help you address those issues.

10

How do you make sure your coaching process will work?

Understanding the variables so you can manage the dynamic

What does coaching involve?

Coaching unlocks people's potential to improve their performance. They don't have to be poor performers to warrant coaching. True, it's often used to resolve gaps between actual performance and expected standards of performance, but it can help develop characteristics with potential beyond their current contribution to competent performance. But let's not skip over that word 'unlocking'. Coaching is as likely to be about removing a block to a latent skill (e.g. challenging and changing a hindering belief) as it is to be about enhancing the way a characteristic works.

Coaching unlocks people's potential to improve their performance.

Coaching can be a one-off related to the development of a specific characteristic or it can be an ongoing in-the-moment way of working with team members. The former is a planned process, while the latter is built around spotting something, intervening with instant feedback (to show them what you've observed is happening) or with a question to change people's perspective and move them forward. You can sustain the impact of informal coaching through monthly review for learning discussions in which you ask a specific question to follow up on any in-the-moment coaching that took place during the month.

We may think we're a constant, but we're not

For a long time, I believed I was the only constant in my tasks and relationships. However, since I learned how differently I react to different people, I now know that I'm the biggest variable. Our beliefs dictate what we notice, how we judge, and the way we choose to interact with people. Which do you value more – professional qualifications or managerial experience? How does that value affect the way you relate to people with the one you value least? Or most? And if you value both equally, how does that affect the way you judge people with one but not both characteristics? My working relationship with Jenny was coloured by the fact that I value more highly people who are straight with me rather than nice to me.

The person you're coaching brings something unique to the dynamic

To coach well, you need to know about your team member's attitude to you, the way they learn, their level of self-awareness, their willingness to develop, whether they are prepared to take responsibility for their own development, and whether the way you coach suits their learning style. Also, you need to know how the characteristic you're coaching contributes to your team member's overall performance, because this will affect the coaching dynamic. As will its role in the job, the importance of it, the extent of the learning need, and the number of situations in which it is used that are available for creating a development opportunity. The person you are thinking of coaching? How much of this information do you know about them?

So does the operating context within which the coaching takes place

This includes everything from the way your normal management relationship with the person you are coaching works to the team and organizational culture within which the coaching takes place. You need to develop a coaching style that's compatible with your general management style – if you suddenly shift from task-oriented, tough manager to person-oriented, caring coach, your team member will wonder who you are and what happened to their real manager. How far away from a coaching management style are you? Would it be a good idea to think about general changes you need to make before you start coaching? The team and organizational culture surrounding you and your team member can also have an important effect on the dynamic. How much time do managers in your organization have for things like coaching? Are you under pressure to fit people management around getting the task done?

And the way you manage your relationship with them

Successful coaching has two key ingredients that you need to get right – self-awareness and responsibility.

I like the definition of **responsibility** that describes it as '**response-ability**'. Being responsible means that in our moments of choice, we recognize that we don't just have to react, we can respond. It means looking at our options for responding, weighing up the potential consequences of each option, deciding which one will achieve the best results, and responding on that basis.

You need to manage your relationship with the person you are coaching so it's clear where your responsibilities end and theirs begin, and so that your interventions are aimed at increasing your team member's self-awareness.

It's all in the mix – the way the variables come together

No variable works in isolation of the others, so it's important to understand how they impact and reinforce each other. In Part 1, I don't suppose it helped that Jenny and I didn't get on, that we were working on a characteristic that I valued and she didn't, and that we were trying to make important personal changes while working in a high-pressure environment. And, of course, when you alter one of the variables, you alter the whole coaching dynamic.

A different team member – a different way of learning

Different people learn in different ways:

- Some people trust their instincts and just shrug it off when things go wrong. They're bored by routine, repetitive tasks and thrive on drama, excitement **Different people learn in** and anything new. They take an **different ways.** active part in meetings, often contributing more than their share. They're open-minded about new experiences and tend to act first and think second. These people are *event-oriented* and learn best from new experiences and anything with a hands-on approach.

- Some people are life's observers, standing back and watching rather than getting stuck in. They do less than their share of talking in meetings and often make great facilitators. They don't like to be rushed, preferring to get all the facts together before making a decision. These people are *review-oriented* and learn best when they have time and space to think things through.

- Some people need something new to make sense to them before they can do it. They are analytical and detached, and can get irritated with people who lark about. They feel uncomfortable about going with their instinct, so they like structure and format. These people are *insight-oriented* and learn best when they have an input of theory that has a sound basis in logic.

- Some people are life's questioners, needing to know why as much as how. They delve into things rather than accept them as they are. They don't take anything for granted, and they think it's only natural that people should ask questions when they don't understand. These people are *challenge-oriented* and learn best when they can ask questions and are not hurried along to a timetable.

- Some people love putting ideas into practice and are always looking for ways to make things work more effectively. They are practical, down-to-earth people, and they probably subscribe to the idea that those who can do, do and those who can't, teach. These people are *application-oriented* and learn best when there is an obvious link between what they are learning and their job.

Which one sounds most like your team member? And what about you?

And not just one different perspective . . .

Different team members have different beliefs, which lead to different behaviours, which lead to different results, and they bring their beliefs, characteristics, experience, values and pre-programmes to the coaching dynamic. When you coach, you're entering potentially treacherous waters because you're working to raise someone's self-awareness, which might lead them to have to challenge their perception of themselves, the image they believe they portray, or an important coping strategy.

A **coping strategy** is a pattern of behaviour that we use repeatedly as a defence against things we fear we can't cope with. They're habits and, like everything else, can be helpful or hindering depending on the situation, the use you make of them, and the effect they have.

The number-one rule in coaching is no matter how hard we try to give neutral feedback, we can't ever totally escape from our own perspective.

Our **perspective** is basically what we see from the position we are looking at things. Anyone who is in a different position from you (including your team member) is bound to look at things differently. And as our actions are based on our interpretation of what we see and hear, a different perspective will lead to different action.

It helps to remember that everyone is entitled to their own perspective and to assume that your team member's perspective will be different to yours.

But two

We already know that your perspective changes depending on which team member you are looking at. It's a lot easier to coach someone you like and feel at ease with. Much as we may wish it was different, we can't like everyone we work with. Are you the kind of manager who cuts people you like a little more slack? Or are you the kind of manager who is tougher on the people you like and easier on people you don't like, to compensate? Either way, you're responding like a human being to another human being. Don't beat yourself up about it, but be aware of how it impacts on the coaching dynamic.

IN SHORT

- **Coaching is about unlocking potential.** Do you genuinely believe that every member of your team has untapped potential?

- **You, the person you are coaching, and the operating context all affect the way a task is done.** How might things work differently if you analyzed the variables before you coached?

- **Everyone has their own way of learning.** Do you coach others the way you would want to be coached?

- **Your team member will have their own perspective – on their performance and on you.** How is your coaching affected by what you believe your team member thinks of you?

- **You can't like everyone in your team.** What impact does liking or disliking a team member have on your relationship with them?

11

How do you avoid the 'skills focus' trap and build your process around the 'human element'?

Understanding yourself and the person you're coaching

Surfacing your subconscious expectations about performance

Our beliefs generate subconscious expectations that affect what we notice and how we interpret what we've noticed.

> **Subconscious expectations** are pre-programmes that tell us what to expect in certain situations or with certain people.

For example, the team was up against a tight and important deadline. I was giving orders left, right and centre and most people were rushing off doing things I needed doing. Most, but not all. One man was wandering around calmly like the deadline would never come. I was pretty miffed, especially as it was my neck on the block if we missed the deadline, not his. Obviously something didn't meet my subconscious expectations of what a sense of urgency looked like.

Not judging other people by our own standards

We all have a tendency to see someone behave in a certain way and think, 'If I behaved like that, it would be because of this, so if they are behaving like that it must be for the same reason', but it's only guessing and it's more likely to be wrong than right. When I've got a sense of urgency about something, I have a tendency to get a frazzled look, a frayed note to my voice, and spiky hair from running my hands through it a lot.

Not judging people on autopilot

When we're on autopilot, we judge people and situations by first taking in information (observing, listening, etc.). Then we process that information by comparing what we've seen and heard against our subconscious expectations (derived from the pre-programmes we've formed from previous experiences with points of similarity). Then we come to a judgement (based on the pre-programmes) and apply this judgement to the person or situation via our response (often using the same response as we did in the pervious experience we're drawing on). Our RAS then looks for (and always finds) supporting evidence that reassures us that we're right.

Getting off autopilot on to manual – and reframing

How did I do that in my example? I took a deep breath (to smother the urge to yell at him), decided to give him the benefit of the doubt (I always did that with him because I never really warmed to him so I overcompensated), and talked to myself:

- Am I irritated with him because when I have a sense of urgency I rush around so he should too (subconscious expectation) so I believe that if he isn't rushing around he can't have a sense of urgency?

- That doesn't sound very fair. He might be one of those people who looks calm on the surface but, like a swan, is paddling like crazy underneath (challenge subconscious expectation).

- So what's he actually doing? Okay, he *is* standing around but he's got things on the go . . . I hadn't noticed that before . . . and he's just told me everything's on schedule . . . so . . . maybe he does have a sense of urgency after all (reframing).

What I like about this approach is it doesn't expect us to be saints. We still get to start from our autopilot judgement, we just don't get to respond until we've challenged our thinking. Do you know someone who irritates you because they don't respond the way you expect, yet they still do the business, just in a different way to the way you would do it?

Judging effects rather than behaviour

What matters is not how people go about things but the effects they create and whether those effects help or hinder

What matters is not how people go about things but the effects they create.

overall performance. If you judge people on their effects, it will lead you towards analyzing how those effects were achieved. And, as any overworked manager will agree, why waste valuable energy changing something that's not done the way you do it if they're getting the right effects?

Getting out of our own way

Our noticing and judging systems can be less than 100 per cent reliable. Think about first impressions. Do you know someone who judged you on first impressions that didn't do you justice but who never gave you a chance to change their mind? Before you coach anyone, ask what your experience of the other person is telling you about yourself and deal with that first so it's out of the way and you can look more neutrally at the behaviour of the person you're coaching.

Letting your coaching be a lesson to you

In the process of getting out of your own way, you'll learn a lot about who you are – as a coach, as a manager and as a human being. It's tough, but it generates a lot of fellow feeling for the person you're coaching – which is no bad thing.

You're coaching a simultaneously complex and simple human being

There's no getting away from the fact that we are complex beings – full of thoughts, choices, characteristics, actions, results, experience, values, principles, beliefs, pre-programmes, habits, tendencies, coping strategies, defences, intentions and hot buttons. We're also simple – driven by our needs. The way we behave to meet our needs is driven by our beliefs about what behaviour will achieve them. Behaviour can only be transformed by a shift at belief level, and yet all we have to go on as managers and coaches is the behaviour we see and hear.

Whose self-esteem may be wrapped up in a false self-image

In a dynamic, when you alter one variable you shift the whole dynamic, and human beings are a dynamic all of their own. It's impossible to know the basis on which any individual's self-esteem rests or indeed to know how strong or precarious that self-esteem is. We all know people who believe their own publicity – it's not a phenomenon restricted to celebrity; it's just as prevalent in the workplace. I remember coaching an architect on his management skills and asking him about what he did to encourage and motivate his staff. He replied that he didn't do anything, he was just an architect and they weren't taught that kind of thing in university. I asked him what he did to motivate and encourage his children. Our conversation left me feeling that this man's whole identity was wrapped up in his profession and that the fact that he was also a manager, a husband and a father who had learned life skills that made him more than *just* an architect hadn't registered in his mind. In coaching him to do a little less architecture and a little more managing, I was, in effect, asking him to give up the thing on which his self-esteem was based. Remember, there's always a logic, so if someone has a false self-image, you have to accept that their subconscious believes they need it to keep them sane. And, as you can never know what the outcome of any coaching intervention will be, you must work with coaching as a helping process, not a managing process. The person you are coaching must be in charge of if and how they change.

And who may be scared of removing their mask

I say 'if' because we can't change people who don't want to change. I was coaching a colleague recently who saw himself as something of a standard bearer for equalities and had a big passion about people taking responsibility. Sadly, what he saw when he looked at himself was not what the world saw. They were masks he wore to hide the fact that he treated women with appalling sexism and blamed everyone except himself for his predicaments. I was meant to be coaching him on improving his impact and I knew that his impact was poor because people saw (and reacted negatively to) this incongruence. I could also tell that he wouldn't be able to cope with removing the masks and accepting the reality of his behaviour (a necessary prerequisite for change). You can't force people to change if they aren't ready to face what change involves. You have to accept that their subconsciousness knows best and that one day it will have created so many negative experiences that change is the only option left.

And who may not be aware of all their options

I want to labour this idea that everyone has a 'logic' because that's the fundamental shift I'm advocating in the way we coach people. Coaching is about finding their logic and working to help people come to a logic that works better for them. One of the things I find often is that performance is undermined by people believing they have fewer options than they really have. In my example, the manager didn't think he had any other option but to be the way he was. His self-esteem was low and he didn't see the talents he could use to improve his impact. Had he been ready to change, he would have needed someone to help him see those talents and provide emotional support while he learned new ways of relating to people. Every time we make a choice, we are choosing the best of the available options. But what happens when we believe we have Hobson's choice? As a coach, one of the easiest things you can do to help people improve is to offer them options they hadn't thought of.

Every time we make a choice, we are choosing the best of the available options.

Watch and learn – but understand you're only guessing

Think about an able-bodied driver who parks their car in a disabled parking space. What thoughts do you think go through their heads as they do it. 'I'm only going to be a minute', 'I'm in a hurry and the only other space is right across the car park', 'I need to be this close to the shop as I'm buying something heavy', 'This space is always empty whenever I pass so I'm not really putting anyone out', and so on. If you look at their behaviour, what do you think it tells you about their underlying beliefs? Three people could display the same behaviour and have three different beliefs. One may believe equality means no special treatment for anyone, regardless of circumstances, so they have a perfect right to park where they like. Another may believe that disabled parking bays are a good idea but they may believe more strongly that exceptions to every rule should be allowed in special circumstances. A third may believe it's not what you do that counts, it's what you get caught doing. The challenge in coaching is that you can see the behaviour that needs to be changed but you can't see the belief that supports it, yet you can't change the behaviour until you change the belief. You can guess, and good coaches get to know their team members well enough to be able to make good guesses, but you must make sure you don't act on your guesses until you've tested understanding with the person concerned.

Understand the behaviour and you understand the person

It's an outrageous claim, I know, but in my experience, it's true – but only if you see behaviour as the starting point of understanding and not the finishing point. We can't ever know what's in someone else's mind, but we're capable of developing alternative theories to explain the connections in the 'needs lead to beliefs, which lead to behaviour, which leads to results, which lead to experience, which leads to more beliefs' cycle. And we can test our theories with the person we're trying to understand. The point I'm making is this: if you don't try to understand the behaviour, you'll never understand your team member well enough to exert the influence you need to get the results you want.

Find a non-threatening language for discussing behaviour

One of the reasons I like to talk about people as a cast of characters is that it allows me to talk about sensitive issues in a light-hearted, almost caricatured way that makes people feel accepted. It's amazing how much ground you can cover with someone if you don't make a big deal out of their quirks.

Sharing your effort to understand is the best attention you can pay

In my experience, people want to matter for who they are and not just for what they do. They want to be heard, understood and accepted. You don't have to be right in your understanding – you just have to care enough to make the effort, and you'll be surprised how much it moves your team forward.

IN SHORT

- **Don't judge other people by your own standards.** Have you had an experience like mine where you judged someone on the way you'd behave in the same circumstances? If you reframed your experience of that person, would you judge them differently?

- **Judge effects rather than behaviour.** Have you ever been miffed when someone achieved the same results as you but did things differently?

- **Human beings are complex and should be handled with care.** Have you ever, with the best of intentions, rushed in where angels fear to tread?

- **Guess about people, by all means, but don't act without testing understanding.** Have you ever been sure you knew why someone did something only to find out that you got them completely wrong?

▶ **Showing you're willing to make the effort to understand people is one of the best things you can do for them.** How much effort do you put into understanding your team members?

12

How do you ensure the responsibilities are allocated properly?

Shifting from a parent/child to an adult/adult relationship

They are the only ones who see their whole performance

None of our characteristics works in isolation of the others, and each works differently in different situations, so a rounded picture of performance is essential for effective development. And the only person who sees the whole of anyone's performance is the person themselves. Do you think your team members are the same in your team meetings as in their own?

None of our characteristics works in isolation of the others.

The only lasting changes are internal ones. You can (with constant supervision) get changes in behaviour, but as soon as you stop pulling the elastic tight, they'll snap back to their own standards.

They must be willing to see themselves as they are

Before someone can change, they have to be able to look at the experiences they are creating and say 'I did that' rather than 'It was the other guy's fault'. They have to be prepared to lift their masks and see what's behind them, to understand that when someone is pushing their buttons it's telling them more about themselves than it is about the button pusher.

And be committed to raising their performance standards

You'll never make a tidy person out of a slob until they change the standards operated by their internal regulator.

We all have an **internal regulator** that maintains our standards at the level our subconscious thinks is right for us, based on our beliefs about ourselves. Its job is to pull us up to our standard when we slip back and to drag us back down when we get above ourselves. If we don't think highly of ourselves, we settle for lower standards than we're capable of, or we push ourselves to achieve perfection – either way, we feel bad about ourselves. We can't change our internal regulator until we change our beliefs about ourselves.

I have a friend who puts up with a womanizing partner because her internal regulator tells her she doesn't deserve better. I'm using a personal example, but the same applies to work – people do sloppy work because that's what their internal regulator tells them is good enough. If only, as managers, we could raise their standards to match our standards, life would be bliss – but we can't. What we can do is help them to see they're underselling themselves, that they have the potential to do so much more, to build their self-belief so they want to raise their own standards. It's a longer, tougher road (there's no denying that), but the pay-off is that you can transform the performance of your team by transforming what's in their heads.

The trouble with subconscious learning is that you can't be sure what you're learning.

To change, they need to become the best learners they can be

People learn from their experience regardless of whether they do it consciously. The trouble with subconscious learning is that you can't be sure what you're learning. Effective learners regularly review their performance to identify learning points and use the insight they've gained to improve. They develop their learning skills beyond just their natural preferences for certain stages of the learning cycle. Above all, they believe there's always more they can learn. They're not complacent because they know that no matter how effective they are in their job right now, their job will become ever more complex as time goes by so the bar is always being raised.

And maximize their experiential learning opportunities

There are four types of learning experience – two proactive and two reactive. Of the four types, two can be found in existing work and two can be found in new work (the perfect excuse for delegating if an excuse is needed):

- We learn when we react to an event – this happens most often when we find ourselves dwelling on something that's gone wrong, but we also learn a lot from things that go right.

- We learn when we react to a new experience – often the very newness is a kind of mental shock to the system and can start us thinking about what we've learned.

- We learn when we set out to look for the learning possibilities in existing work – we're most likely to be doing this when we start a new job, because that's when we think of ourselves as 'still learning', but effective learners do it all the time by looking at their job with fresh eyes.

- We are actively looking for new experiences so we can learn something new – when we're so comfortable in our existing jobs, we feel we want to be stretched by a new challenge.

And manage their own learning process

Obviously, you can't make someone learn something that they don't want to learn. What I have noticed, though, is that people feel more comfortable with change when they're in control of it (have you noticed how we never resist the changes that were our own ideas?) so it makes sense for them to manage the review for learning process. That includes getting the best out of you as a coach.

You focus on creating a good coaching environment

You can do this by being more open about who you are so there's not one rule of openness for them and another for you.

Talk about your characteristics and tell them where they work for you and where they don't. I've been doing this for years and it doesn't make my team respect me less. And the added bonus is that I don't have to pretend to be the perfect manager – they know I'm human and they cut me slack when I need it, just like they would in any other adult/adult relationship.

What do you think of the idea of everybody in the team being a coach? It teaches people how to observe behaviour and give feedback, and it breaks up some of the barriers that happen in hierarchies without upsetting the basic chain of command. It's also an excellent way for people with a special skill to contribute to the team.

On analyzing their performance, giving feedback, and helping them learn

We all need to see ourselves from another perspective from time to time. Your feedback on your team members' performance can help them see, for example, how a characteristic they've judged as a weakness helps them in some situations. Your normal management routines, such as holding monthly reviews for learning sessions, can help them learn from their experience. Your wider knowledge of the organization and upcoming changes that might cause a new competence gap can help too. And the attention you pay to the things that matter to their performance will focus their attention on the same things.

Help them get clarity – listen to articulate

Most people know what they have to do differently; sometimes they just get so bogged down in the complexities of the situation that they lose sight of their own solution. One of the best ways I know of helping people when they're stuck is to listen to what they are saying and just feed it back to them. And no, I don't mean that touchy-feely therapist 'I'm unhappy', 'you're unhappy' reflecting back. Listening to articulate is listening for the meaning in the muddle of what they're trying to say and feeding it back to them in a more articulate manner than they've given it to you so it makes more sense to them than it did when they said it. It's more than reflecting – it's translating I suppose.

Hold them responsible for their own development

Too many management books tell you it's your job to develop your staff, but, fundamentally, the responsibility for anyone's development lies with them. You can, and should, help but you can't do it for them. Someone talking about EQ (emotional intelligence) once said that the greatest act of caring we can do with someone is to hold them responsible for being their best self. And that's the manager's role in development, just as it is in management.

Be detached, fair and committed to doing your best for them

To do all this, you need to be able to get out of your own way, treat everyone fairly, and be committed to doing your best for them. That last point isn't the same as helping because sometimes the best way of helping someone is not to help them.

You need to be able to get out of your own way, treat everyone fairly, and be committed to doing your best.

There's a real self-discipline to helping effectively. Too often, helping in the short term hinders in the long term. Managers who save their team members from the consequences of their mistakes prevent them from having an experience they needed to learn from. So resist the temptation to rescue.

Be willing to challenge yourself

I focus a lot on the need to help people challenge their hindering beliefs because that's a major aspect of improving their performance. But the same applies to us as coaches. There'll be times, when you're coaching, when you'll hit the brick wall of a hindering belief of your own, and that's when you need to be willing to take responsibility for your own development. Remember that next time you feel like giving up on a team member, because you may discover a belief that some people are un-improvable and, for a coach, that's the most hindering belief of all.

IN SHORT

- **The only person who can develop you is you, and the same goes for your team members.** Do you ever inadvertently take over your team members' responsibility for developing themselves?

- **People will develop only if they want to raise their standards.** Have you ever wasted your time trying to develop someone who was capable of more but happy with the way they were?

- **The best learners make the best performers.** On a boring training course where you're learning nothing, do you just sit back and bemoan the waste of time or do you try to make it work better for you?

▶ **Make it easy for them to take responsibility**. Do you mother your team members? Have you ever let compassion stop you making the right choice?

▶ **Coaching teaches you a lot about yourself**. Do you have any beliefs that might undermine your performance as a coach?

13

How do you choose an area of performance to improve?

Observing and analyzing behaviour to pinpoint development needs

Looking for effects that could be more helpful to performance

Start by asking where you'd like to see better results. Your first choice for coaching will doubtless be to fill gaps between actual and expected levels of performance, but you can also look for unused potential. As you think about performance, think about what you're actually seeing and hearing. Be careful not to judge – don't, for instance, decide that a person is not managing their time well enough because that's an interpretation. Note what you've actually observed – that their work often misses the deadline, for example, or that they often appear harassed and rushed. Judging too soon can get you hurtling off down the wrong track. I remember a manager telling me about a problem in his department. He called it a skills mis-

Start by asking where you'd like to see better results.

match, which he believed came from the fact that his department was moving into a new type of work and his staff were trained to do only the old work. I asked him to tell me what he actually saw, and he talked about poor-quality work, missed deadlines, some work not getting done at all, and so on. I kept probing, but there was nothing in what he was actually observing in his department that led specifically to the skills mismatch judgement. Do you have a performance problem in your team that you've already given a label to? Why not follow these steps and see where they take you?

Separating characteristics from factors affecting performance

The next step is to brainstorm as many possible contributory factors that could cause the effects you've observed. The more possible causes you come up with, the better, as they will form your framework for further observation. Divide the causes into two types – characteristics and factors affecting performance. Characteristics are all the things your team member brings to their performance, while factors affecting performance are those things beyond their control. Remember: this is not a black-and-white judgement thing. Most causes will be due partly to characteristics and partly to factors – so when other people don't do their bit, that's partly a factor beyond your team member's control and partly a reflection of their influencing skills. If in doubt, apply the test of reasonableness (would it be reasonable to expect someone to have that factor under their control?). My colleague with the skills mismatch had his eyes opened when he'd finished his two lists, as most of the items were on the factors affecting performance list (such as poor

If in doubt, apply the test of reasonableness.

direction, expected performance not made clear, communication poor), with very few items on the characteristics list where you might expect a skills mismatch to show up.

Going back for a second look

So far, you've identified possible contributory factors of the effect you are observing, but to see which ones are actually contributing you need to observe again. This time, use your analysis as a framework for your observations – because this time you're looking for evidence to support or counter each of the possible contributory factors you've identified. At this point, it is not unusual to discover that all the contributory factors are factors affecting performance rather than characteristics. This means you need to take off your coaching hat, put on your manager hat, and sort out the factors. Supposing, however, you find that in a missed deadlines problem there is evidence of poor time management and coordinating skills? Well, now you know which characteristics you're working with.

Observing the same characteristics in more helpful situations

To help someone turn a characteristic that is hindering performance into one that helps it, you need to know more about that characteristic than just how it operates when it's hindering performance. You need to think about (and if necessary observe some more) how your team member uses that characteristic in helpful situations so you can come to an overall perspective on whether it's a strength (more helpful than hindering) or a weakness (more hindering than helpful). Getting this rounded picture is essential because you want to improve the way it's hindering this particular area of performance but without undermining its contribution in other areas.

The value of getting a rounded picture of performance

If this all sounds too hard to bother with, remember two things:

- You're wasting both your and your team member's time if you get the wrong analysis. This is like the planning stage of a project – the more you invest now, the less time you'll need later.

- If you can get to a point where you really understand your team member's performance, giving feedback becomes easy. You'll know exactly what you're talking about and have the examples to back it up (which will enhance your credibility with your team member no end). And you'll have the perfect antidote to the dreaded sandwich feedback technique because you can talk about the characteristic in the round – showing where it's helpful as well as where you'd like to improve it.

IN SHORT

▶ **Working carefully through the behavioural analysis process will pay dividends later on**. How often do you watch your team members perform and try to understand their performance?

▶ **The more acutely you can observe performance, the better the quality of feedback you can give**. If I asked your team members about the quality of your feedback, what would they say?

14

How do you give feedback and come to a shared understanding of the issues?

Giving neutral 'cause and effect' observations and agreeing development needs

Making neutral statements that describe your observations of cause and effect

For feedback to be credible, it has to be stated in a way that a neutral observer would have stated it, not as a frustrated manager who's fed up with missed deadlines might say it. It sounds easy to describe exactly what you saw in terms of behaviour and effect, but how much easier it always seems to give a judgement like 'you got angry and frightened her' than to observe 'you raised your voice with your team member and she sank back into her chair and her face went pale'? On the plus side, with the neutral statement you're not giving them anything they can argue with. In the example about missed deadlines, you might say something like:

You've missed the deadlines for the last three pieces of work from the finance department. I've noticed that in the middle of working on the task, you stop to open emails as they arrive and deal with people who stop by your desk or ring you rather than ask them if you can get back to them later. I've also noticed that you don't do any of these things when the deadline is for a customer, with the result that you meet your deadlines on those occasions. So I was wondering whether you'd noticed the same thing and what causes the differences in your approach?

Getting into the right frame of mind to give feedback

It's not easy to give neutral statements of cause and effect (especially on something like missed deadlines, where you probably had to deal with the fallout yourself), so it's important to be in the right state psychologically. It can be very calming to remind yourself:

- My aim in giving this feedback is to help, so I need to remember that it's not about making them feel bad but about generating a useful discussion about how to improve.

- The focus is on what they need to know to improve their performance, not on how I feel.

- No matter how detached and objective I've tried to be in my observations, I am still giving only my perspective and I need to stay open to alternative perspectives that may be equally valid.

I think you get my drift. I'm labouring frame of mind because if your attitude is solid (neutral, wondering and not judging) and if people believe you're sincere, then you can mess up the words you use and still do a good job of giving feedback. But if

If you don't actually feel judgemental, you won't sound it. you feel judgemental but use neutral observations, then your team member will pick up the incongruence on a subconscious level even if they don't pick it up on a conscious level. If you don't actually feel judgemental, you won't sound it, whatever words you use.

Sometimes feedback is all that's needed

Obviously, as this is a book about coaching, I'm writing about feedback as one step in a bigger process, but it's worth noting that sometimes the simple act of raising someone's awareness about an issue is all you have to do to improve performance. If, by giving feedback, you've brought something to your team member's attention that they hadn't realized was happening, resolving the issue might simply be a matter of them watching out for a bad habit until they've replaced it with a good one.

Giving feedback as part of coaching

There are six occasions when you may need to give feedback during coaching.

- When your team member doesn't understand what they are aiming at, and when they aren't clear what competent performance in a particular characteristic is.

- When they lack self-awareness and don't see themselves clearly enough to improve their performance.

- When they're being too self-critical or when they're focused narrowly on one interpretation or perspective.

- When you can see a hindering belief that's holding them back.

- When they're not motivated to change, tempted to revert to old ways, or in need of appreciation for their efforts.
- When they're not learning from their experience.

Get the feedback right and the rest falls into place

If you get off on the right foot by getting the neutral description statements of cause and effect right, the rest will fall into place. Your team member will respect your objectivity and see your sincerity in wanting to help, and you will have given them enough solid information to kick-start a discussion that will get your team member thinking and analyzing rather than reacting and defending.

Using feedback to kick-start the analysis process

Although feedback can be an end in its own right, it's more likely to be the beginning. Done well, it creates the right atmosphere (neutral and wondering rather than judging, analytical rather than defensive) for a good discussion on performance. In the example I gave earlier, the feedback ended with a question to invite analysis. It's a simple technique, but it works due to our conditioning at school to answer questions. The aim is to get your team member to do the actual analysis with you asking questions to challenge thinking and listening to articulate when they're muddled.

Explore in rich narrative form to surface subconscious intentions and beliefs

To come to a shared understanding, you need to know the person's insight into the issues. A simple 'tell me what you think' will usually be enough to get your team member talking. People like to tell their stories to an interested audience (yes, even when it's the boss). While they're doing that, you need to be listening out for anything that doesn't make sense to you (logic plus intuition). Let your subconsciousness do the work while you ask questions to get behind the story to the meaning. All you're trying to do at this point is to find your team member's logic and maybe any options they considered and rejected so you know where their choices came from.

To come to a shared understanding, you need to know the person's insight into the issues.

Coming to a shared insight about performance

The storytelling allows your team member to get things off their chest so they can focus in a more analytical way. This is especially important if they are feeling defensive. Defensive behaviour is usually associated with feeling attacked, so if you're in neutral mode you may not be expecting it. But, remember, people may still be defensive even when you're not judging them, because they're either judging themselves or they've got years of experience that's generated a subconscious expectation about being judged. If you think there'll be a lot of emotion in the discussion or that it'll be sensitive in some way, it can be a good idea to have the 'tell me about it' part of the discussion before you give your feedback. You can then include your feedback in the main analysis part of the discussion.

(This is why I dislike the idea that you can take a step-by-step-process approach to people management. With most people, feedback first – to make your point and get their attention – will work well, but there will always be exceptions. The best advice I can give is to have a process in mind but adapt how you put it into practice based on what you know about your team member.)

The next part of the discussion is about the characteristics (knowledge, attitudes, behaviours, skills) that were factors in the performance. You'll have done some thinking on this yourself as part of your observations, but what you need is for your team member to decide what needs to change so they are committed to doing it. Here's an example relating to the missed deadlines problem from earlier.

My insight was that my team member seemed to like keeping all the plates in the air at the same time, making a bit of progress on each rather than focusing on the ones with dead-lines. He agreed that he tried to keep all his projects moving along, but his insight was that he'd prefer to work on one project at a time. He just didn't think that was an option in his job. I was surprised at this (I thought it was his natural style), but we came to a shared insight about the frustrations caused by his preferred way of working being at odds with his actual way of working.

Consider alternative perspectives and other feedback

It's always worth considering how things look to anyone else involved in the incidents you observed. In my example, what did his team members think of the way he worked, and how did they feel about the team missing so many deadlines? Also, important as your feedback is, it won't be the only feedback your team member gets, even if it's the only *formal* feedback. It's important that you surface any other feedback your team member has got and help them analyze that as well.

> By **feedback**, I mean any signs we pick up about reactions to what we're doing. It's not just the formal feedback we get when the boss reviews our work; it's all the little signals we don't necessarily notice consciously but that our subconscious picks up and uses to adjust our thinking, behaviour and actions. We get feedback all the time regardless of whether we think we do. Without it, we'd never know how to adjust the course to achieve our intentions.

Challenging hindering beliefs

Once you've got a shared insight, you can look at the beliefs at the heart of the problem. My team member believed that making some progress on all projects was what was required and that the only way to achieve deadlines was to adapt to the dictates of the job. To me, this was a hindering belief as I thought it was possible to meet project deadlines and work more in his preferred style. I suggested a diary management system, where he could carve out blocks of time for single-project working. This reflected my belief that jobs should be shaped to suit the person doing them, not the other way around. Sometimes

Once you've got a shared insight, you can look at the beliefs at the heart of the problem.

challenging hindering beliefs is all you need to do because, in some cases, seeing things differently is all that's needed to do things differently. In my example, though, we needed to look a bit more closely at how to match performance to the new belief.

Analyzing characteristics

We looked at his characteristics and agreed to focus on his diary management skills and his attitude to being interrupted by his team. There's a lot more on how to do this later. What I need to say here is that this stage of the process is about coming to a shared understanding and that doesn't stop just because you've reached a shared insight about what the issues are. It applies to the analysis of characteristics so make sure you ask your team member where they think the characteristic is helpful and where it is hindering. Remember, they are the only ones who see their whole performance.

Once you've analyzed the characteristics and know what's actually happening in performance, you can start planning the right development opportunity.

IN SHORT

▶ **There's no room for judgement in feedback.** How neutral are you when you give feedback?

▶ **Even neutral statements of observed behaviour won't work if you are feeling judgemental because people will always spot your incongruence.** Are you genuinely neutral or just playing at it?

▶ **Always end feedback with a question to generate discussion.** How do people respond to your feedback? With discussion or defensiveness?

▶ **In the end, it's their analysis that counts not yours.** Do you ever succumb to the temptation to win the point rather than win the person?

▶ **Poor performance is often the result of a hindering belief.** Do you stay on the surface when you are improving someone's performance, or do you get down to belief level, where you can make a transformational difference?

▶ **Even if you sort beliefs, you'll still need to be able to analyze characteristics.** How self-aware are your team members? Could they analyze their own performance and identify their characteristics?

15

How do you help them create and manage a development opportunity?

Applying the homoeopathic development method

Agree competent performance and scope for development

The starting point is to agree what you're both aiming for, which is competent performance. There's more on this later, but the important point to make here is that your team member must have their own clarity about what competent performance is. They need to know what the results will look like – both outputs and outcomes.

We produce **outputs** (things) to achieve **outcomes** (results). The trouble is, we're often so focused on the outputs that we lose sight of the outcomes, yet we exist to deliver outcomes not outputs. There are always more outcomes than you think, and many are unintended. In the diary management example, there was an unintended and unwanted outcome to do with poor relationships within the team, who felt it reflected badly on their productivity.

Then they must track back and identify what they need to be able to do to achieve the outputs and outcomes. This focus on inputs is essential because factors beyond your team member's control will often affect the outputs, so you can't assume that poor outputs reflect poor inputs, and so you need to be able to assess performance separately from results. In my diary management example, my team member and I agreed that competent performance would be:

- *Outputs*: the diary for the week ahead would show blocks of time clearly allocated to projects, with meetings being fitted in around these.

- *Outcomes*: no deadlines missed.

- *Inputs*: my team member would plan his actual week's work rather than just his week's meetings (which in the past had left him trying to fit his hands-on work into the time left over) and ease his team members into a new way of working to replace the interruptions.

Agree development objectives

A development objective describes the characteristics someone needs to be able to bring to their performance. It can describe the outputs as well (which often gives a focus to the learning), but it must be capable of being assessed in isolation of results that may have been affected by factors other than the characteristics of your team member. If your team member

A development objective describes the characteristics someone needs to be able to bring to their performance. writes up the development objectives, it gives you a way of testing understanding and gives them a feeling of ownership. Development objectives for my team member's diary management development need were something like this:

■ To be able to assess the time required to progress projects in any particular week, schedule that time into the diary, and be self-disciplined enough to stick to the plan.

■ To be able to deal assertively with interruptions in a way that does not detract from either the attention to project work or the management of the team.

Bear in mind that you're not trying to write down every aspect of competent performance in the characteristic you're developing. You're only trying to describe those aspects that your team member needs to develop. So, there is no standard diary management development objective – it will be different for different people with gaps in their diary management performance.

What's a homoeopathic development opportunity?

A little of what kills you cures you so long as it's very diluted and the dosage is managed properly (apologies to homoeopaths for my amateurish interpretation) is, in my experience, the ideal way to develop people. So for my team member we worked up an approach to developing his ability to manage his diary and staff interruptions that he could actually put into practice in his job on a day-to-day basis.

Helping them create a development plan that starts from where they are

This is essentially a discussion about how the characteristic can best be developed. In the example of diary management, we talked about the need to break down the change required into smaller parts. So at first, my team member decided to take himself off into another room to work on projects – which meant that he didn't have to worry about handling interruptions until he'd got into the swing of working for long periods on one subject. Even though it was his preferred way of working, it had been so long since he'd done it that he needed time to adjust to it. Besides, his old way of working had brought some gains that he was ambivalent about losing – he's sociable and can feel isolated when working solo for long periods – so he needed time to deal with them. We talked about other ideas and agreed he'd try one thing at a time to see which ones worked best for him.

Build a good radar system

The next step is to design a radar system.

A **radar system** answers the question, 'What information do I need (in what form, at which points, after what triggers) to know whether what is supposed to be happening is actually happening?' It's about giving you the feedback you need to intervene and take action to either put things back on track or change the track.

In the diary management example, all we needed was an interruptions log and for my team member's diary to show what he actually did with his time as well as what was planned. We used the results from the radar system as a basis for reviews for learning, so we had hard data to analyze as well as perceptions.

Take it one step at a time, build slowly, and review for learning regularly

My team member got into the swing of solo project working, and when he was comfortable managing interruptions he'd be able to do the work back in his own office. Small changes that can be incorporated into the job one piece at a time work best. And, given that this is experiential learning, each small change needs to be accompanied by a review for learning, because all change is a chance to surface more issues.

IN SHORT

- **You can't achieve something you can't visualize**. Are you absolutely clear about what competent performance is for your team members? Could you describe it to me if I asked you to?
- **Focus on developing what people bring to their performance, and the performance will improve**. Do you focus on what they produce or what they produce it with?
- **You can't manage without a radar system**. What lets you know when something isn't happening the way it should?

16

How do you ensure they learn and use what they've learned?

Managing learning and the journey to unconscious competence

We're always learning whether we're conscious of it or not

Something happens. We review the event – most people do this on a subconscious level, but to avoid risk of misinterpretation making time to do it on a conscious level is crucial. We gain some insight – again, if we don't make sense of the event consciously, then our subconscious will lay down a programme for us anyway. Then we challenge our previous insight – sometimes the event and the insight we gain force us to re-examine an old belief before we can absorb the new one. Then we apply our new insight to our future experience – usually in a trial-and-error way, learning more as we go.

We can do this process subconsciously (such as in going on a training course and just expecting new ways of working to happen as a result of attending), but the trouble with that is that we aren't conscious of what we're learning so we have no control over whether we're learning the right things. Our learning can be affected by the way we subconsciously interpreted the event and, if we misinterpreted, we can learn things that will hinder future performance. If we learn consciously,

Our learning can be affected by the way we subconsciously interpreted the event.

using the review for learning process and making sure we go through all the stages so we don't block ourselves, we've a much better chance of learning things that will help our performance. As a manager, I know which approach I prefer my team to take, and I make it my job to do as much as possible to ensure they do, which is why my coaching includes regular reviews for learning. Reviews for learning raise learning to a conscious level and encourage completion of the full learning cycle, so that learning can be applied to future experience.

Be prepared

In a review for learning, preparation means thinking about and making notes against the standard review for learning questions.

I regularly do **reviews for learning** with my team – sometimes one to one and sometimes with a whole project group, depending on the issue. We prepare by considering the following questions first on our own and then together:

■ What went well and what went less well? What did I do to contribute to the outcome? What do I know now that I didn't know before?

- What have I learned about behaviour (about myself, the way other people behave, etc.)? What insight have I gained about dealing with this kind of experience in the future?

- To enable me to use what I have learned, what, if anything, do I need to challenge about the way I think or the way I behave? Are there any old ideas or behaviours that I need to unlearn first?

- How, where and when can I use this insight to improve my performance?

At this stage, these notes are intended for personal use in the discussion because sharing them in advance encourages defensiveness and inhibits the quality of discussion. The aim of the review is to come to a shared understanding about your team member's performance.

They talk, you listen and ask questions

The questions are only a way into thinking about the experience under review and a way of giving structure to the discussion. It's the follow-up questions that really open up the discussion. What follow-up questions? I can't tell you that because you need to work those out for yourself by listening carefully for anything that, for example:

- Skates over the surface of a point that could bear further examination.

- Seems to contradict an earlier point.

- Says more by what it implies than what it actually says.

What you hear will generate your questions. 'Can you tell me more about that?' is one of the most open questions you can get, so ask it a lot. And try to ask questions that make your team member think, as opposed to questions that ask for a yes/no answer or a piece of information.

Helping them extract all the learning points

Your aim is to help them get as much learning out of their experience as possible. If you're anything like me, you'll be itching to get in there and offer them your insight, but try to restrain yourself. It's the intervention of last resort, as your insight is always going to be external (and therefore less likely to effect a change), whereas if they can get their own insight you have a potential transformation on your hands. Your main role is to look for blocks to learning and see what you can do to help move them forward (more on this later).

Conscious competence is the high-risk stage

While a new skill or way of behaving still requires a conscious effort to sustain it, there are risks that people will slip back into their former ways. We all have lapses –it comes with the territory of being a human being – particularly when we're under stress, when our autopilot sends us back to the way we know best rather than the way we know *is* best. Investing time in your team member at the conscious competence stage will help ensure that they get to the unconscious competence stage.

There are risks that people will slip back into their former ways.

So ensure the learning cycle is continuous

To take something on board as a new way of working requires many trips round the learning cycle, adjusting as we go – it's a continuous process. Something happens, we review it, learn from it, challenge our old thinking, apply what we've learned, experience it in a slightly different way, review that experience, learn a bit more, challenge a bit more of our old thinking, and so on, until we are well and truly in the comfort zone with our new way of working.

Get into the habit of monthly performance reviews for learning

If you change only one thing about the way you help people improve their performance, make it finding an hour of your time once a month for each of your direct reports to help them review their experience. It allows you to follow up on previous learning and development action (by asking how they're using what they've learned), and it allows them to bring experiences to the discussion that weren't necessarily part of a development plan and discuss them with you. The review for learning is a simple way of ensuring that your team members learn from their experience, and it provides opportunities for you to use a coaching approach outside of any formal coaching processes you have going on with that team member.

A monthly performance review for learning works on the same basis as an ordinary review for learning (it still takes people around the learning cycle) – it's just not restricted to looking at one specific experience, it's looking at the whole month under review. The questions I use in my monthly reviews are listed below, and you're welcome to use them as they are or adapt them to meet your needs.

1. What have you achieved, and how does it compare with what you planned to achieve? How do you explain any variations? How well have you managed your time across your different work areas and priorities?

2. What was your best and worst performance, and what is your analysis of each? What challenges have you faced, and how have you managed them?

3. From whom have you sought feedback on your performance (e.g. employees, colleagues, customers)? What have you learned from the feedback?

4. Overall, what insight have you gained from your experience over the last month, and when/how are you going to apply it in future? What do you need to challenge about the way you think/behave at present in order to apply your insight effectively?

5. What have you done since our last meeting to develop yourself, to apply what you have learned, and generally to improve your performance?

6. What do you plan to achieve next month (both task and development activities)? What support do you need, and from whom?

I'm trying to build a feedback culture so I devote a question to that to show it's where I'm focusing my attention, but you can always substitute questions that ask about issues that matter to you. I find six question areas is about the maximum you can discuss in an hour, so don't go above that unless you're prepared to devote more time to the review. The answer to question 6, once you've agreed it, becomes part of the answer to question 1 the next month, so it keeps the cycle going forward. I like to use their answers to question 1 to make sure I appreciate results that may have been overlooked at the time.

Give feedback all the time, and the sooner the better

Feedback is an excellent way of reinforcing helpful behaviour and raising awareness of hindering behaviour. And if you get your management style right, you don't have to worry about all the stuff they tell you in the books about giving feedback. In fact, on the contrary, you can best develop a feedback culture by ignoring what they tell you in the books. Let me share my experience.

Feedback is an excellent way of reinforcing helpful behaviour and raising awareness of hindering behaviour.

I've always worked under the kind of pressure that made taking people to one side and giving feedback privately (recommended standard operating procedure in all the books) a bit of a luxury, so for a long time I just let the moment pass without giving feedback. Nowadays, I break all the rules, but it works. The minute I see something I need to feed back on, I give it there and then and I don't worry about who else hears. But – and this is a big but – I do it with humour and no judgement and make a point of ensuring everyone knows that I take people to one side only if it's something bad. This does four things that really make a difference to the team culture:

- It makes people see open feedback as a good thing (because private feedback is the time to worry).

- When I do take them to one side, it saves me having to labour the 'you're in trouble' point.

- They are comfortable giving each other (and me) feedback because it's just part of the culture.

- We're all open about our own characteristics and accepting of each others.

Adapt the job to make more use of new skills

You can help bed in new ways of working by giving your team member new tasks that make use of them. Delegation is an excellent way of doing this. A note of caution though. You need to remember not to 'reward' good behaviour with more work as that might seem more like a punishment than a reward to your team member. My rule in this – as in most things to do with people management – is if in doubt, ask them . . . and remember to be in doubt more often.

IN SHORT

- **Conscious learning is the only reliable way of improving performance**. How much of your learning is conscious, and how much is subconscious?

- **Formal reviews for learning can be a way of building the learning habit**. How often do you sit down with your team members and help them learn from their experience?

- **Knowing how to do something and doing it automatically are two different things**. How much ongoing support do you give your team members when they are mastering a new skill?

- **Give feedback to reinforce helpful behaviours and challenge hindering ones**. Do your feedback behaviours help your coaching efforts?

- **Give them chances to use what they've learned.** How do you manage this tricky issue?

PART

3

■ *real* management for the way it is ■

Knowing when to help during coaching

▶ **Give them what they need to adjust course**

We all adjust course on the basis of feedback, so if you don't give
it they'll get it from somewhere – or they might assume that no
news means they're doing okay when they're not. It's not fair to
let people carry on going down the wrong track when you can
say something to help them get back on the right one.

▶ **Don't just take my word for it –. check it against
your own experience**

As you read this part think back to a recent coaching experience
and review it against what you're reading.

17

When don't they know what competent performance looks like?

The need to help them get clarity about what they're aiming for

Get them to do the work – to get their subconsciousness in on the act

Nothing beats getting your team member to do their own research on this – and no, that's not just because it saves you time (although that's an additional benefit). The more absorbed they get in finding out what competent performance is, the more their subconscious will switch on their RAS to help them notice it when they see it. You can help by giving them some pointers to get them started on their research.

- Get them to look through flyers for training courses – course outlines can give clues to what they think competent performance looks like (ditto books).

- Get the team together for a brainstorming session on what goes into making competent performance of that characteristic – many heads are better than one on this as it taps into a wide range of different experiences.

I'd like to focus the rest of this chapter on a few of my favourite ways of getting clarity about competent performance. They're favourites because they build the team member's observation and analysis skills so give double benefits.

The good, the bad and the ugly – watching other people perform

The first thing is simply to watch other people perform, see where they're using the characteristic in question, look at the effects they're having, and analyze how they're achieving those effects. I especially like doing this with characters on television – okay, so I'm a sad person whose work is also her hobby, but it's the only kind of interaction I can observe where I'm not also expected to make a contribution.

Anyway, clearly we're not picking out an expert performer in this exercise to benchmark against so your team member will see lots of examples of people using the characteristic in different ways and with varying degrees of success. This is great because they will get a really rounded picture of how the characteristic works and how it doesn't, which will help them when they come to develop it in themselves.

Looking at poor performance to see how not to do it

Because, sadly, it's often easier for us to see what's wrong with other people than what's right with them, it can be good to pick someone who is really hopeless with this particular characteristic and analyze what they're doing wrong to pick up the cause-and-effect behaviours your team member wants to avoid.

Interviewing star performers

Think of someone who excels at the characteristic and get

Think of someone who excels at the characteristic and get your team member to ask them how they do it.

your team member to ask them how they do it. Don't worry about people making time to talk about how good they are at something – oddly enough, it's never a problem. Ask them:

- What was your best ever experience of using (the characteristic)?

- What was good about it? (Ask follow-up questions so they tell you in rich narrative form.)

- What was the most important thing, the one thing that really made the experience what it was?

It's always useful to have one eye on the performance dynamic

When your team member is doing whatever research you've agreed, they need to bear in mind that no one characteristic works in isolation – it works in a dynamic with other characteristics. It's useful for them to observe what else is going on at the same time so they can see the bigger picture. It's all too easy to get focused on being a better listener, for example, and forget that listening used without questioning to test understanding and to probe for more details is only half as effective.

Don't forget the review for learning

Learning from other people's experience is the only fast-track learning method that works (because it's still learning from experience) but, as with any experience, your team member will learn from it only if they review, find the insight, challenge their old thinking, and so on, so don't forget to do a review for learning with them on their research experience.

Learning from other people's experience is the only fast-track learning method that works.

IN SHORT

▶ **Don't tell people what competent performance is; help them find out for themselves.** Do you tell, sell or ask?

▶ **Performance is a dynamic so they need a narrow and wide focus when they're observing other performers.** When you're watching someone to learn from them, do you focus narrowly on their skill *and* widely on how it integrates with the rest of their performance?

▶ **You can't learn from what you don't review.** Have you ever done a review for learning on someone else's performance?

18

When are they lacking in self-awareness?

The need to help them see themselves more clearly

First they have to be looking in the right direction

There are many reasons why people lack self-awareness. One is that we don't actually look at ourselves. How many of us stop and review our experience on a regular basis and really see the effect we have on others? In an overworked world, we're lucky if we get a chance to catch our breath between one task and the next, never mind time to review it.

How many of us stop and review our experience on a regular basis.

And then they have to be willing to see other people as mirrors

Do you remember me saying that Jenny's wimpish streak pushed a button in me and that I've only just realized it was because I have a wimpish streak of my own that I deny? Well, if I'd been the manager at the time of that example that I am now, I'd have seen my over-reaction to Jenny for what it was – the fact that she was being a mirror to my disowned characteristics. What I'm saying is that as long as we let our reactions to other people tell us more about them than about us, we'll never become as self-aware as we need to become to improve our performance.

And then they have to see what's in the mirror

The other reason people lack self-awareness is they look at their performance but just don't see parts of it. In other words, they have a blindspot.

> The idea of a **blindspot** (the technical term is scotoma) has been borrowed by psychologists from the field of ophthalmology, where it means a situation in which part of a person's visual field just does not work. The person can see everything else, but they can see nothing in the area of the scotoma. And they cannot know what it is they aren't seeing. They are 'blind' to the 'blindspot'. In the field of psychology, it refers to a mental blindspot, where a person is simply unaware of their own role in creating a particular experience.

Have you ever known someone who had no idea why people were unfriendly with them but it was completely clear to everyone else? I always know when I've discovered one of my blindspots as I go round telling everyone in the team about my eureka moment and they all act like it's yesterday's news – which to them it is because they knew it all along.

And interpret it correctly

The big problem here is our RAS, which, as you know, ensures we see only what will reinforce our beliefs about ourselves. It takes time to get used to operating with your intuition on full alert for what feels 'off' and start noticing things that don't fit your beliefs as well as the things that do. We need to look out for signs that our team members are misinterpreting the events that happen to them.

How do you know someone isn't self-aware?

There are lots of clues to lack of self-awareness in others if you know where to look:

- Watching them repeat the same mistakes is one way of knowing.
- When they get feedback from other people that they just don't 'get' is another.
- Or when they're producing poor results on autopilot, reacting on instinct.
- Or when they can't explain their own logic.
- And when they can't answer when you ask them for their three most helpful characteristics and their three most hindering ones (or three strengths and weaknesses if they still operate in the old ways).
- And when they can't analyze their performance or when their analysis leaves out something obvious.
- Especially when there are discrepancies between their view of themselves and how other people see them that they can't explain except by saying people have got them wrong.

- When they're telling you about someone who's pushing their buttons and you know that they have the same characteristic.

You can – and should – help them become more self-aware

How do you do that? No prizes for guessing – by giving neutral statements of what you have observed and the effect you have observed (a.k.a. feedback) and leading the discussion towards an analysis. A good way of helping people find their blindspots is to get them to think of someone who pushes their buttons and explore what it is they do that pushes the buttons, then find examples in your team member's own behaviour of the same kind of thing.

And when they finally see it, they need to believe it – which takes time

When you're helping someone become more self-aware, remember that it takes time to come to terms with who we are, and that the more false our picture of ourselves is, the more time it takes. You can't just hope to move straight on to the next step. However gentle you are, you're doing a tough thing, so give your team member time to let go of their old picture of themselves. Changing their inner picture is the hardest thing anyone can do, so we should allow time and space to adjust.

> **When you're helping someone become more self-aware, remember that it takes time to come to terms with who we are.**

IN SHORT

▶ **There's no easy way of raising someone's self-awareness, and there can be no development without it.** Do you take the hard road or the easy one when you're faced with a lack of self-awareness that is hindering a team member's performance?

▶ **You have to know they're lacking in self-awareness before you can do something.** Are all your team members highly self-aware individuals? Are you?

▶ **People need time to come to terms with new insights about themselves.** Have you ever been so psyched up to give someone bad news about themselves that you plough on, regardless of whether they're coping well?

19

When are they being judgemental instead of analytical?

The need to help them get into neutral and consider other interpretations

No one can judge and analyze simultaneously

Judgements are fine when they come after careful considera-tion, but not when they are a knee-jerk reaction to something not going the way we wanted it to. Our analytical and judging functions are separate – the theory being that judging follows analysis, the practice often being that judging comes first, with analytical skills being used to support or rationalize the judgement. Knowing that people can't do both simultane-ously means you can stop them doing one by getting them to start doing the other. How do you do that?

Get them to tell you the story

You knew that already, didn't you? Here's an overview of the approach I take.

- They come to the table with their minds made up.

- I ask them for the story of the event, which makes them go back to the beginning. Getting the story in 'rich narrative' form often gives me a real feel for what went on, especially when I use questions to get past the interpretation to the neutral observation. For example, my team member says they made someone angry, and I ask, 'What did you actually say, and how did he react?' to get back to what really happened and check their interpretation.

- I ask them to analyze the cause-and-effect relationships that led to the negative outcome on which they are judging themselves so harshly. This distracts them from judging.

- I then ask them to consider different perspectives, which broadens their focus away from themselves as the centre of attention – which we always do when we're feeling bad about ourselves.

- I hunt for counter evidence or things in the situation that don't support the judgement – by listening for what doesn't seem to fit with the rest of what they are saying.

- I try to find one good thing in a bad situation – not to make them right when they're wrong, but to get a more balanced judgement. If they've done something wrong, they've done something wrong – this is not a whitewash technique, it's about coming to a considered judgement.

Now, let's pick up a few of those points in more detail.

Getting them into neutral

You can't make progress with people who are beating themselves up. And even if they did a terrible thing, and you think they ought to be beating themselves up, they can't learn while they're doing it so it doesn't actually move anyone forward.

Tackling their RAS

When people are fixed on one way of looking at something, they won't see counter evidence. Your job is to get them to look specifically for things that don't fit with their interpretation of the event. If they think everything is a disaster, push them to find one good thing to come out of it. They'll struggle against the idea, but persist and there's bound to be something.

If they think everything is a disaster, push them to find one good thing.

Reframing and rejudging

You can try getting them to imagine that the event had happened to someone else that they were observing and ask them what it would look like to them. Would they still judge it in the same way? Often, people judge themselves in ways they'd never judge anyone else, so this helps get things in proportion. Get them to look at it with different eyes – how do they think the person on the receiving end saw it (and if they catastrophize, get them to justify by showing evidence from the reactions of that person).

Leaving them upbeat and looking forward

Sometimes we feel bad about an event because we've done something that would have upset us if done to us, so we assume it's upset the person we did it to. But everyone is different so this isn't a reliable assumption. Working with your team member to get into neutral and to reframe, isn't just about moving them away from premature black-and-white judgement into proper analysis so that the ultimate judgement is more rounded. It's also about moving them away from being emotional about the event into thinking rationally about it.

> I want to distinguish **emotions** from **feelings**. Emotions are mental states (coming from our thoughts) and feelings are physical sensations. Emotions can generate feelings, as with anger and a tight feeling in the chest, but they are separate. The same feeling can be associated with two emotions – for example, a churning stomach can be fear or excitement depending on our thoughts about the situation we're in.

Ultimately, your team member may be right in their judgement, but this exercise will stop them feeling so bad about their mistake. And if they still feel bad, you can focus them on making amends by getting them to think about how they can retrieve things.

IN SHORT

▶ **People can't judge and analyze at the same time.** Tell the truth. How often do you conclude first and rationalize afterwards?

▶ **Our first conclusions about events are not often our best.** How often have you reframed an emotionally challenging event when you calmed down?

▶ **If you don't leave people upbeat, they will associate change with pain.** How do people come out of coaching sessions with you?

20

When are hindering beliefs holding them back?

The need to help them remove blocks to achieving their potential

Get them to tell you the story

I know I keep saying that (and I'm beginning to wish I wasn't old enough to remember Max Bygraves), but it really is the only way to go. It takes more time, of course it does, but it's worth every minute you both invest.

Articulate what you're hearing

I've already raised the idea of listening to articulate. When I talked about it earlier, it was about translating something you got from your team member that was fuzzy and unclear and giving it back to them in a way that was clearer and made sense to them – as their sense, not yours. What I'm suggesting here is using the same technique but with the things they are telling you by implication rather than explicitly. It's about articulating the meaning of what they're saying. It's not about them being fuzzy. On the contrary, some of the most articulate people I know (who'd never need translating in that way) are the most unaware of the implications of what they are saying (where do you think tactlessness comes from – never fuzzy, but never meant the way it's taken?).

Suppose a team member is telling you the story of a customer who complained about something that hadn't been done and became very rude when your team member explained why. Somewhere in the story, you begin to sense your team member believes that customers care about supplier problems (and maybe they do, in a parallel universe) and you think that belief has hindered your team member's performance. You simply articulate that belief in a testing understanding way: 'It sounds to me like you believe our problems matter to our customers and I can see how, if you believe that, you'd think they'd want to know why we haven't done what they want. Am I right in thinking that?' You'll be surprised how quickly the air clears once you've done this. Sometimes, articulating a belief can be like feedback – all that's necessary. In the example above, as soon as I'd suggested the belief my team member was operating on, she saw for herself how unlikely it was and she changed her approach pretty quickly.

Explore the impact of the belief on the results

Once you've articulated a belief, the next step is to explore the cause-and-effect relationship – that is, how the belief affected the behaviour that produced the results. It's not rocket science – I'm guessing you've already made the connections in the example above – but it is important to get it out in the discussion as it's an important step towards developing alternative beliefs.

Develop and try out alternative beliefs

To help someone develop an alternative belief, you need to challenge their existing belief. Common sense is when something appeals to our conscious and subconscious minds so your challenge has to appeal to both. We all know how to make a reasoned argument to challenge their logic, and you can challenge their intuition by asking them about the various experiences that led to them having that belief and listening for negative experiences. You'll notice just how much evidence there is of negative experiences to call upon to support your argument that the belief doesn't produce the desired effect. In the example of the customer not interested in excuses, what their belief led my team member to believe would happen did not happen. In fact, quite the opposite happened, as is often the case with hindering beliefs.

Common sense is when something appeals to our conscious and subconscious minds.

The aim of this exercise is not to rubbish their beliefs; it's to open them up to other possibilities. And once you do that, you've got them out of judging mode and into analytical mode. Just ask them to imagine being a neutral observer looking at the results to work out what they are telling them. So, in my example, 'Customers don't want excuses, they want results' might be an alternative belief.

Rehearsing the new belief to see how it works

It's not just a matter of finding a new belief to replace the old one. It's also about letting them try it to see whether it fits while you're there to help them if it needs adjusting. I get them to 'walkthrough' the experience again.

A 'walkthrough' is when someone rehearses an event in their head by describing, in storytelling detail, what is happening from start to finish. It's a bit like doing a running radio commentary on a fantasy football match. It allows you to anticipate potential problems and other people's reactions and to be sure that you haven't missed anything.

But this time they have to behave as if they believed the new belief instead of the old one. The 'walkthrough' shows your team members that an alternative belief creates an alternative experience.

IN SHORT

▶ **Sometimes people can't see the sense they're making because they're too close.** Have you ever experienced someone making more sense to you than they do to themselves?

▶ **An alternative belief will create an alternative experience.** Have you ever helped someone see something differently by challenging their belief?

21

When do they need motivation, encouragement and appreciation?

The need to provide emotional support without becoming a crutch

It's all about building inner strength and independence

Personal change is tough and it's not always pleasant when it suddenly becomes clear to someone that they've been getting it wrong for years. When people judge themselves harshly for behaviours done in a time of lesser self-awareness, it can often lead to a lack of self-belief in their ability to change. They are at a vulnerable stage, and the way you handle the times when they need emotional support can make the difference between them becoming dependent on your good opinion and becoming strong through generating their own good opinion of themselves.

Your aim should be to build their inner strength and self-belief so it's self-sustaining. If you avoid praise and criticism (both judgemental behaviours) and stick to neutral feedback, it teaches people to look at their own performance and judge it for themselves. It's important that people get a clear idea of what their own standards are so they aren't tossed about by feedback (good and bad) of people with their own agendas. It's a tough world out there and we all need to know for ourselves when we've done a good job. I've seen people destroyed by the opinion of others because they've taken it as a truth instead of an opinion and they've had nothing in them to counter it so they've just soaked it up like a sponge. It's a lifetime task for most of us to build our self-esteem to a point where we're resilient in the face of other people's criticism. A few months ago, I gave the first few chapters of my first book to someone to read. He savaged them and, even though I've had a lot of compliments about my writing over the years, it took me three days before I could read them again and say to myself, 'Hey, they need work but they're not that bad – he's obviously got his own agenda, so trust your own judgement girl.' Helping people get to the point where they can do what I did is one of the best things one human being can do for another.

Aim to build their inner strength and self-belief so it's self-sustaining.

Don't *try* to motivate, encourage and appreciate – it never works anyway

I've tried more methods of motivating than I care to confess, and none of them work – and no, it wasn't just me! The only kind of motivation that sustains people comes from inside them and, quite frankly, if they're not feeling motivated you can't make them feel motivated so there's no point trying – especially as trying often makes people feel even more demotivated. I'd steer clear of encouragement too, not least because it's hard to do it without inadvertently invalidating their feelings ('I can't do it', 'Yes, you can' – see what I mean?), which only makes matters worse. And finally, expressing appreciation in a way that isn't meaningless, patronizing or both – well, it's a minefield as I'm sure you know only too well.

Just tell them what you see and let them do the rest

So, either we keep trying to motivate, encourage and appreciate and go down fighting, or we carry out our responsibility for providing emotional support by doing something different. I've found what works consistently well is to tell people exactly what I see – but only after I've put time, care and attention into my observation and analysis of their performance and the effects they are achieving. In my experience, people feel most appreciated when they feel noticed, much more than they do with even the most fulsome praise. When my input is factual, they take it and use it to adjust their perception for themselves. It's not an instant transformation; it requires mulling over, but I've sown the seeds of a different perception and that seems to be enough.

Point out where there's been progress

One thing I tend to do a lot when I'm providing emotional support is to use the techniques described elsewhere in this book. I diagnose the problem and give the appropriate help. So, if they're discouraged and I think they're judging themselves too harshly, I follow the route in Chapter 19. If they're demotivated because they are creating negative experiences through a hindering belief, I follow the route in Chapter 20.

When I want to show my appreciation, I simply follow the route in Chapter 14 and give straight feedback focusing on everything they did well and how I thought it contributed to their results. If they're not glowing with pride by the end of my factual, almost journalistic observer type exposé of their brilliance, I add a rider about how pleased they must be with their performance (which I mean sincerely, but which I'm also aware can soften even the most self-critical heart).

Always start from where they are

The other thing I do – apart from using feedback – is to start from where they are and not where I think they should be. So, for example, I take their feelings of discouragement as fact rather than perception and help them solve the problem that's causing them to feel discouraged. If their discouragement is results-based (things not actually going well), then the problem solving is focused on practical things. If it's

Start from where they are and not where I think they should be.

come from a misinterpreted event, then the problem solving is focused at belief level. I try to resist the temptation to tell them they shouldn't be discouraged or demotivated, but I don't fall into the touchy-feely trap of telling them it's okay to feel those things either (on my planet, there's such a thing as overvalidating people's feelings and encouraging them to feel like victims).

If in doubt, ask – and be in doubt a lot more often

We're all different, with different needs for emotional support at different times, and the only way we can be sure we're getting it right is to ask the people we're supporting. Sometimes the best solutions *are* the simple ones.

IN SHORT

▶ **Creating independents is better than creating dependents.** Do people come to rely on your praise to keep them going?

▶ **Don't invalidate people's feelings, even (especially) if you think they're over-reacting.** Do you inadvertently fall into the trap of telling people they're wrong when you're trying to be supportive?

▶ **If in doubt, ask them – and be in doubt more often.** How often do you just 'do as you would be done by'?

22

When are they not learning from their experience?

The need to ensure they complete the whole learning cycle

People can become blocked at any stage of the learning cycle

Getting all the way round the learning cycle isn't as easy as it sounds. People can become blocked after:

■ The event stage, when they go from one experience to another without reviewing their experience and therefore without learning from it. These are likely to be people who operate on instinct (subconscious) without necessarily understanding their own logic. Just slowing them down through having reviews for learning with them will be enough to get them to reflect.

■ The review stage, when they can get stuck dwelling on what happened and not make it to the insight stage. Then they'll feel bad about things that go wrong but never learn how to put them right.

■ The insight stage, when they get stuck because they don't challenge what they need to unlearn. They just try to add new knowledge to outdated knowledge instead of having a clear-out of beliefs that no longer make sense.

- The application stage, when they learn everything but don't apply what they've learned. They are the ones who know when they've made a mistake but keep on making it because they're comfortable with their old behaviour.

Assuming it's a blockage and not a deliberate act

I don't think believing that people are lazy, thick or just generally awkward is a helpful belief in the context of coaching. I'm going to assume that you're reading this because you want to be a good coach to your team and, if you had that belief at some point in the past, you don't have it now. The reason it helps to assume there's a learning cycle blockage is that it gets you into neutral analyst mode and gives you something to look for when you're analyzing why they got stuck. I learned from one of my team members, who gives up when he doesn't think there's an answer for him to find, that always assuming there's an answer is a great empowerer (if there's such a word) in problem solving. And when someone isn't learning from their experience, believe me that's a problem.

Asking the right questions to discover where they're blocked

Once you know someone is repeating the same experience and getting the same negative results, you need to ask questions to find out which point in the cycle they're stuck at. Just work through the following list and see where they answer 'no'; that's where they've hit a block:

- Have you reviewed your experience of [whatever the bad results are]?

- Does that tell you anything you didn't know about your performance?

- Has your thinking changed in any way since you had this experience?

- Has your approach or behaviour changed in any way since you had this experience?

Once you've found out where they're blocked, a review for learning will take them round the rest of the learning cycle.

They might have completed the learning cycle but not got all the lessons

The other likely problem is that people are going round the learning cycle but misinterpreting their experience, and thus learning the wrong things. The team member who had the problem with the customer may have reviewed his experience and come to the conclusion that he was right in his approach and that it was just a difficult customer (you won't be surprised how often that kind of interpretation happens). Sooner or later, when his subconscious has recreated the same negative experience with many more customers, he might do a review for learning and come up with a different answer, but why wait? When a team member isn't learning from their experience, it's our job to facilitate their learning.

When a team member isn't learning from their experience, it's our job to facilitate their learning.

Remember there can be blocks at different depths too

I keep saying that human beings are complex, but it does pay to remember that when you're looking for blockages. People may not be learning from their experience because they:

- Are afraid to change or are too comfortable as they are.
- Don't know any other way, so this is the best they can do.
- Don't see the results they're creating as negative.
- Think it's the other guy's fault and they're the victims of circumstances.
- Don't have the skills to analyze their performance.
- Don't have the self-awareness to see how they contribute to a situation.

So, remember that you might not just be looking for problems at the level of behaviour. You might also be looking for blocks at the level of beliefs and needs.

IN SHORT

▶ **People aren't stupid when they don't learn from their experience, they just don't complete the learning cycle properly.** Do you try to get to the bottom of why someone isn't learning as they should, or do you just judge them?

▶ **People who complete the learning cycle may still not learn the right lessons.** Have you ever found out the hard way that doing the right thing didn't please your boss and end up learning to do the wrong thing?

■ *real* management for the way it is ■

Conclusion

▶ Leaving the hard sell until last

Most management books start by selling you the benefits of their approach, presumably to motivate you to actually try it. It seems more sensible to me to assume that you're already motivated to want to try it, otherwise you wouldn't have bought the book. The question is, have you stayed motivated while I've explained how complex life in the real world is?

▶ Do you want the benefits enough to face up to the complexity?

Not sure? Then read on . . .

23

Why should you persevere with *real* coaching when it's so complex?

I can't answer that, I can only tell you why I persevere

Only you know why you bought this book and what it would take to motivate you to try some of the ideas I'm putting forward. All I can do is tell you what motivates me to coach and what I get out of it.

Coaching changes the culture

Coaching helps create a high self-awareness and high-feedback culture. The people in my team (myself included) do not only know their own characteristics; we know each others' characteristics and we talk openly about them amongst ourselves. There'll always be irritations and issues between people in teams. I've worked in teams where people talked about each other behind their backs as a way of venting their tensions, and I'd choose the way our team does it any

Coaching helps create a high self-awareness and high-feedback culture.

day – we tell people what's pushing our buttons, but we use humour. Having a really good belly laugh with someone releases the same amount of tension as getting angry – unlike politely stating your grievance, which leaves the anger nowhere to go. When you work in a high-pressure environment, you need ways to release the tension. Taking a non-judgemental, coaching approach to management generally and to people's development needs in particular can ease the tension enormously.

And builds capacity for the future

It's comforting – and secretly pleasing for the ego – to know you've created a team whose performance standards are high and who are capable of dealing with whatever the job throws at them. You can coach on all the tasks that are on your team member's current job so it complements the work you do with your team when you delegate.

Experiential learning is faster, cheaper and more focused

I've done my share of sending people on training courses only to be disappointed when they came back full of ideas but no application (and that's from the good ones!), and I know how much better learning is when it's based on real work experience. Once you get the hang of coaching, it becomes easier and easier to see the learning points in every experience and you can bring people on in leaps and bounds because you've got so much experiential learning material to work with.

Coaching gives you and your team member the confidence to delegate

Delegating one of your tasks to one of your team members is a risky business, no doubt about it, but the more competent your team member is the less risky it is. When you coach, you can see close up what your team member can do, and you can work on the areas that undermine their performance. And that kind of knowledge makes deciding what to delegate to whom a whole lot easier.

And there's always self-coaching

It's easier to be a neutral observer when you're coaching someone else than to be your own neutral observer, but DIY coaching can be done and it's a lot easier if you regularly practise your skills on your team. Once you've got the hang of reframing, for example, you'll find it an invaluable tool for managing and developing yourself. And, let's face it, if you wait for the boss to coach you, chances are you'll be waiting a long time!

Above all, it's a chance to hone your observation and analysis skills

The skills you use for coaching aren't just useful for coaching; they're essential for effective performance in everything you do. It sounds horribly self-centred to describe coaching as a chance to practise your observation and analysis skills on your staff in a safe environment where you are in control but, hey, it's true, so what can I say? Your team members aren't the only ones who get to develop their skills when you coach them, and there's a lot to say for self-interest as a motivator.

I hope that even if you don't try coaching straight away, you'll try observing people's behaviour and trying to find their logic. I know what it's like to be overworked and undervalued (I'm guessing you're familiar with that scenario – am I right?), and I know how much better my management performance has been (and how much easier my life has been) since I stopped judging and started really looking and wondering about what I was seeing.

If you do the same, you'll be only a short step away from being a great coach and a great manager.

Appendix 1

Towards a way of managing for the new era

The beliefs that help me make sense of my world and the people in it, including me

Beliefs come before action – and inaction

Columbus had to believe the earth was round before he could set sail to prove it, and the same applies to us in everything we do.

People do what makes sense – even when you can't tell from their results

How many times have you reacted to someone's actions with 'But that doesn't make any sense'? We can believe human beings are irrational, or we can believe they do what makes sense but that everyone's 'sense' is different. It's easier to make sense of what people are doing if we stop thinking our logic is *the* logic. Have you ever wondered why you did something that got the opposite effect to what you wanted, even though you knew all along what would happen?

If we were conscious of everything we know, our logic would be clearer to us

Sometimes, a new experience that has similarities to an earlier experience will trigger something from the vast store of experiences we keep in our subconscious. When we do this with people, it's prejudice – literally prejudging them based on previous experience that might or might not be relevant. Have you ever taken an instant dislike to someone, then, when you got to know them, liked them? What triggered your initial response? Did they remind you of someone else you didn't like?

Our subconscious mind alerts us through our intuition

When our subconscious mind wants to tell us there's something we've forgotten that's relevant to the situation we're currently in, it uses our intuition. Have you ever listened to someone saying something that sounded logical that you still felt absolutely sure was wrong yet couldn't explain how or why?

Except when it skips that step and drives us straight to a knee-jerk action

Taking an instant dislike to someone is an example of our subconscious bypassing the intuition alert stage and driving us straight to a response. When our responses don't seem logical to our conscious minds, we fear being irrational. But as I said, people always have a logic – it just isn't always a conscious logic!

We don't fail, we just achieve an intention we didn't know we had

Have you ever tried to give up a bad habit and failed? Did you blame lack of will-power? If your conscious and subconscious minds have conflicting intentions, your subconscious will win because it's stronger. What might you have to gain from not giving up your bad habit? Or what might you have to lose from giving it up?

Our needs drive our intentions and our beliefs drive our behaviour

Our beliefs tell us how to behave to meet our needs. Like everything else we've ever learned, we learn our beliefs from our experience. What are you not doing that you know you should because you believe it will be a painful experience?

Our experience is created by our subconsciousness

There's a lot of rubbish talked about people creating their dis-ability, which is a hurtful mistake people make who don't real-ize there's a difference between an event and an experience. Have you known two people who were at the same meeting (event) to describe it so differently (experience) that it was as if they'd been to different meetings?

Which always has its own logic – even when we can't see it

One of the main functions of our subconscious is to keep us feeling sane. The lengths it will go to is probably why it's often called the creative subconscious – as in creative accounting maybe! It governs everything, from the things we notice in the first place – have you ever bought a new car only to start seeing that model everywhere you go? – to the way we interpret events to create our experience.

Our logic comes from our beliefs

My logic will make sense to you only if we both believe that the same (a) causes the same (b). If you believe that smoking causes lung cancer but I believe there's no connection, then we'll never agree on why there's rising incidence of lung cancer among people in developing-world countries who are encouraged to smoke by unrestricted advertising practices, because we'll be analyzing using different logics.

Our ingrained beliefs stem from childhood experiences of pain and pleasure

We form many of our beliefs in childhood, which is a pity because that's when we're worst equipped to interpret events. For one thing, we're dependent on our parents to meet our needs, which means we learn to associate pleasure and pain with how they react to the way we behave to get our needs met. As adults, we can say, 'Well, that's one way of looking at it, Dad, but it's not the only way', but as children, if a parent reacts like we've done a bad thing, we've done a bad thing, and that belief stays with us until something forces us to re-examine it, if it ever does. What's your most painful childhood experience? What has it taught you to believe?

We use those beliefs to interpret later experiences

As a teenager, I got to stay up past my bedtime analyzing history with my mother. And whenever I was upset about anything, she would tell me to pull myself together and try harder. I learned that brains were 'in' and emotions were 'out', and that if at first you don't succeed, try harder and never quit. For many years, I was more Mr Spock than Captain Kirk, and I genuinely believed that my worst experiences were those when I acted on my feelings, not my logic. What about those childhood beliefs you've just identified – do they still influence the way you interpret events? (For anyone concerned for my mental health, I've cracked the 'emotions are OK' thing and I'm working really hard on giving up my stubborn refusal to quit even when I'm flogging a dead horse. I'm not there yet but I'm not going to quit until I succeed. Oh dear, maybe I'm not doing as well with that one as I thought.)

And we learn to judge ourselves according to the feedback we get

My British history teacher used to give me A+ and read my essays out to the class, praising my 'delightful prose' (oh, the shame). My European history teacher used to give me C– and suggest, caustically, 'A few more facts and a little less verbiage wouldn't go amiss.' Do you have a behaviour that's admired by some and criticized by others? In judging it, whose views matter most? If you ignored what others think, how would you rate it?

But other people's judgements of us often tell us more about them than us

I bet you learned more in the last example about my history teachers than about me. What about the people who admire and criticize your behaviour? What do their judgements tell you about them?

So we need to learn to reframe

When I lived in Brixton, I saw a poster with two photographs on it – the first was a narrow-angle shot of a black man running along a crowded street with a white policeman running after him; the second was a wide-angle shot showing both the black man and the policeman chasing a third person. It was challenging people who assumed that the black man in the first shot was a criminal, rather than a plain-clothes policeman, and showing them that they were seeing what their prejudice wanted them to see, not what was there.

When is a strength a weakness? The times it doesn't work for you

Are you sceptical about the things I'm saying? Is scepticism a strength or a weakness? When someone has to anticipate negative reactions to their proposals, scepticism can be helpful. When they're responding to radical ideas from team members by dismissing them without consideration, it's probably a weakness. How we judge a characteristic often depends on what our experience of it has been. Have you found scepticism generally helpful or hindering in your experience?

Competence is often a matter of being a round peg in a round hole

I'm not saying we don't have strengths and weaknesses. I'm saying they're just a reflection of how well we fit our operating context. My favourite ever boss was widely acknowledged as a visionary, brilliant strategist and future 'youngest ever' managing director. Yet although he'd been a good enough middle manager to get promoted, there'd been nothing to indicate how exceptional he was to become. In a middle management 'implement other people's strategies' role, he was a round peg in a square hole, but in a director role, he was in his element. What were your best and worst jobs? How did your characteristics fit your best job, and how were they a mismatch in your worst job?

To get our interpretations right, we have to slow down our judging process

Taking a more neutral approach doesn't mean no judging. We need to make judgements to move forward. What worries me is the speed with which we leap to judgement and the fact that, once decided, we lay our judgements down in our subconscious, start to live by them, and forget to take them out for review. And once we've made a judgement, our RAS ensures we see only things that reinforce the rightness of it (the sanity thing again). Given these consequences, it doesn't seem unreasonable to spend a bit more time wondering and exploring before we judge.

And take the time to listen to ourselves

Whatever we're doing, we're doing two things in parallel. Our conscious mind is doing the activity and our subconscious mind is watching us do the activity, making sure our actions are in line with our intention and triggering alarm bells when they aren't. Listening to our alarm bells is the one sure way we have of staying on the right track.

It's not just characteristics that are neutral, it's events

A friend who'd been in the same job for twenty years was made redundant. He said at the time it was the worst experience of his life. Now he says it was the best thing that ever happened to him because it made him stop, take stock of his life, and think about what he really wanted to do. And now he's doing it and he is happier than ever. Did the event go from bad to good? No, his interpretation changed. It's natural to judge events quickly. It gives us closure (what a yuk word), which allows us to move on but which also stops us learning everything the event has to teach us. Have you ever had a bad experience that you later believed had been good for you?

And emotions

Speaking as a former Mr Spock, I'm fascinated when people describe emotions as bad (anger and hurt) or good (happiness and love). Emotions exist to tell us something about an event. Anger, for example, is triggered by someone breaking a rule that we live by or trampling on a value we hold dear. Assuming we've interpreted correctly, anger tells us to put something right that's gone wrong. It's not our emotions that get us into trouble, it's our autopilot responses. Have you ever used anger, in its righteous indignation form, to right a wrong?

And pre-programmes

I have a pre-programme about consultants that says they come into the organization, talk to staff, write up our ideas (the ones our managers wouldn't take seriously when we told them), present them back to our managers (who now take them seriously because they heard them from an expensive suit), and walk off with a small fortune. My autopilot response to this pre-programme involved saying as little as possible to them. Recently, though, I've worked with a number of consultants who've not fit my subconscious expectation. Pre-programmes can be valid at the time we lay them down in our subconscious minds, but times change and we forget to bring them out and check to see whether they still hold up. Do you have a pre-programme about a group of people that you formed years ago? Are you sure it's a true reflection of your current experience of that group?

And even beliefs

Do you believe in the 'do as you would be done by' golden rule? Have you heard George Bernard Shaw's riposte: 'Do not do unto others as you would they should do unto you. Their tastes may not be the same'? As someone who likes to know where I stand with people, it took me a while to realize there are people who'd rather not know – if where they're standing is a bad place. The golden rule can be helpful as a last resort with strangers (a kind of 'if in doubt, do as you would be done by'), but there's no excuse for being in doubt with your staff

– just ask them! Have you ever done as you would be done by and got short shrift?

The difference between the 'push' and 'pull' approaches to managing change

When we're consciously trying to change something (I'm trying to give up interrupting people), we're in push mode, trying hard, working from our conscious mind. When we give up trying to force change and set our intention on being different (being a better listener), and then just observe ourselves in action, we bring our subconscious mind on board and it gently 'pulls' us towards our new intention. Have you ever set your heart on something impossible, not really worked on it, but still found all sorts of help coming your way?

We need to listen to our fears

We live in a world governed by 'feel the fear and do it anyway' sound bites. Well, let's forget the twenty-first-century pop psychology culture for a moment and think about why we have a fear mechanism. Fear is part of our survival instinct, designed to prepare us for fight or flight. It's there to tell us we need to act. If we don't listen consciously to our fears, our subconscious will listen and sabotage our efforts anyway, so we might as well.

And to the people who push our buttons

For years I've been irritated by status-conscious people. It wasn't until I looked back and realized I'd left one job when the organization became open plan and I lost my office and another because some people on my level were regraded to a higher level that I discovered a status-conscious streak I'd denied for years. What irritates you in other people? When do you display the same characteristic? If you don't believe you have it, ask someone you trust whether you have it before you dismiss what I'm saying.

And to our characteristics

Most people focus on their weaknesses and take their strengths for granted. A friend of mine counted listening as a strength, so he listened more than talked in meetings. His boss (who could win an Olympic medal for talking) branded him a poor performer because he didn't make much impact. If my friend had spent more time thinking about how his listening hindered his performance, he might have done something to improve his performance in meetings. What might you do differently if you really listened to your characteristics?

And to the standards we set ourselves

We all have an internal regulator that maintains our standards at the level our subconscious mind thinks is right for us, based on our beliefs about ourselves. What are your standards on tidiness at home? Do you feel you have to tidy up when visitors are due? Or do you always tidy the mess they make as soon as they've gone? If we don't think highly of ourselves, we settle for lower standards than we're capable of, or we push ourselves to achieve perfection – either way, we feel bad about ourselves.

And to the lessons in the experience we create

I had a colleague who believed all men were sexist. Whenever they used the masculine gender as a catch-all for both sexes, she'd tell them to say 'He stroke she'! They made fun of her and she ended up with a negative experience. I preferred to have fun at their expense. I was fond of saying things like 'I'm a man of my word' and watching their reaction – which was comical. By taking their position and exaggerating it until it became funny, I made them think about language without making them feel bad about themselves and in doing so created a different experience of them.

So we can find the beliefs that help and hinder us

Sometimes our beliefs are buried so deep in our subconscious we don't even know we've got them. Looking at our experience can tell us what we believe. Remember that bad habit you failed to give up? If I asked a neutral observer, 'What must my reader believe (about themselves, others, the world at large) to have created the experience of failing to give up that bad habit?', what would they say to me?

We all have an internal cast of characters

I guess even the most sceptical of us would accept that different relationships and different situations bring out **different 'sides' to our character**. I like to think of the 'sides' of my character as characters in their own right because it helps me keep a sense of humour and be less self-critical when I do

> something daft. Each of your characters represents a need that won't go away just because you ignore it and is often associated with a cluster of characteristics you don't use any other time.

I have a friend who's a real monster at work but completely henpecked at home. Another friend runs her own company but turns into a clinging child when her partner is going away on business. And a middle-aged friend who has a 'rebellious teenager' streak who likes to drink twelve pints on a Friday night even though he can't take his drink like he used to. I have a 'repressed child' character who pops out and emotes at people when my feelings are being ignored. Who's in your cast of characters? What provokes one of them to make an appearance? Which ones do you like, and which ones do you try to ignore?

And a dark side that can shed great light on our performance

Whatever you want to call it, we all have a person we're afraid we might be but hope we're not. We have two tactics for dealing with them – if we're conscious of them, we hide them by wearing masks.

> A **mask** is something we pretend we are to cover something we are pretending we aren't. I have an arrogant streak I don't much like so I wear the mask of openness about things I'm not good at. It has a positive effect on others (they become open too), so I think of my mask as the positive side of my arrogant streak.

If we're not conscious of them, we project them on to other people. What characteristics don't you like about yourself? What masks do you wear to cover them up? How do your masks help you? How do they hinder you? Who gets to you in ways they don't get to other people? Which characteristic of yours might you be projecting on to them?

And coping strategies – though some work better than others

How do you cope with criticism? Do you get angry and defensive, or do you listen politely and then ignore it or feel hurt or rush to explain yourself or criticize the person right back or sulk for a few days then do something about it? If you listen, take on board what's useful, ignore the rest, and feel good towards the person doing the criticism, I probably picked the wrong example for you. I'd like to meet you, though, as I've never met anyone who doesn't use a coping strategy for criticism. What kinds of situations do you not like dealing with? What coping strategies do you use? They protect you, but do they have negative effects?

We influence others by acting out our subconscious expectations

My former colleague acted out her subconscious expectation of men being sexist through her attitude and behaviour, and their subconscious responded to what she was giving out. Many organizations have so many rules that they create a sub-conscious expectation that managers should act like parents and treat their staff like children. As an adult, I don't expect anyone to check whether I've cleaned my teeth, so how come at work we spend so much time checking the work of our staff? The more we act like parents, the more we are acting out our subconscious expectation that our staff will act like children, and the more we will create that subconscious expectation in them. No wonder we don't get excited by the prospect of empowerment programmes. If you empower children, it's all freedom and no responsibility. How do you treat the people you manage? Do you trust them to get on with the task or check up on them all the time?

And they let us – by transferring their power to us

In an organizational hierarchy, people tend to act on their subconscious expectations about authority and power. So, staff expect the manager to know the answers and, in doing so, give away their power and help sustain parent/child relationships.

We also influence by the way we reward and sanction the responses we get

I once knew a woman who could win medals for red-penning reports. Whenever one of her team wrote a report that didn't read well, instead of giving it back to them to rewrite or coaching them, she rewrote it herself. What do you think her team members were learning? What do you do when someone produces a poor-quality piece of work? We don't just reward poor performance, we punish good performance. I know someone who gives all his rush jobs to the person he trusts most. Some reward! What happens in your organization to managers who do good work?

What we focus on expands – so we need to choose carefully

When I wanted my direct reports to improve the way they managed their teams, I started asking them questions about their people management at our reviews for learning. It was amazing how much more they had to report as the months went by. Have you noticed that the better you become at something, the more of it you do? The same thing happens when we focus on our fears. They expand and our subconscious thinks our intention is to avoid the fear becoming a reality.

We can't solve problems with the same beliefs that created them

One of my team had to design a fifteen-day training programme, which more than 3000 managers would be attending. He said it couldn't be done as with those numbers it would take years. It turned out he was thinking about training people in groups of twelve. I suggested we think about the problem not as training but as event management and we ended up with a conference-style approach that allowed us to train 200 managers at a time in a large venue with lots of facilitators. When was the last time you were stuck? What part of your thinking had to change to allow you to move forward?

And we can't change behaviour until we've changed the beliefs that underpin it

Behaviour is so influenced by beliefs there's no point trying to change behaviour. All that happens when we do is we set up a clash between our conscious mind (which is managing the new behaviour) and our subconscious mind (which is trying to keep us sane by getting us to continue behaving in accordance with our beliefs). Think about a bad habit you've successfully given up. What beliefs had to change before you could give it up?

It's our unquestioned beliefs that lead to autopilot behaviour

Our bad habits tell us a lot about the beliefs we need to question. Think back to that bad habit you're trying to get rid of. What were the underlying beliefs? How long have you held them (how far back does your bad habit go)? How many times during that time have you reviewed them to see if they still hold true?

Asking the right questions transforms behaviour by transforming beliefs

Thinking is simply the process of asking ourselves questions and answering them. The trick to good-quality thinking is asking the right questions. I did a course with some twenty-year-olds. We had one lecture with a different case study every week. The lecturer shouted out the questions and we'd shout back with the answers. Everyone thought they could analyze a case study because they could answer the questions. But the lecturer asked different questions for each case study and the trick to analyzing the case studies was in knowing the right questions to ask – but no one was focusing on learning from his questioning skill. Have you ever argued with someone and been unable to change their mind, only to find that when you stopped arguing and started asking them questions they changed their own mind?

If we want to create positive experiences, we have to sweat the small stuff

People don't judge us on the big things; they judge us on their experience of us. We are much less about our major triumphs and disasters and much more about the person we show ourselves to be in those small moments of choice that happen countless times a day. Sweating the small stuff means thinking of the effect you want to achieve and the consequences of your actions before you make choices so that you make your choices – you don't let your choices make you. What makes you decide whether you admire someone?

And get off autopilot on to manual

Just because our brains like being on autopilot doesn't mean we should let them. People aren't machines. Press the key on the computer keyboard that says T, and T is what you'll get every time. Speak to the same person in the same way two days running and, if their mood or circumstances are different, you will get a different response on day two than you got on day one. Does this tie in with your experience?

Appendix 2

From strengths and weaknesses to characteristics

Getting into neutral to exploit all the possibilities

One of the concepts that's most prevalent in traditional management thinking is that of strengths and weaknesses. I know how hard it can be to break out of that kind of thinking so I've included some examples showing how to reframe strengths and weaknesses into characteristics that help in some cases and hinder in others and how to give them more neutral labels if they are needed.

Strengths

- *Decisive* This can be a help when it comes to situations requiring fast and sure action but it can hinder in situations where options need to stay fluid, so I reframe it as 'a preference for a firm and decisive response'.

- *Good listener* This can be very helpful when it comes to facilitating situations or making people feel good about themselves, but as it's not possible to listen and talk at the same time it can hinder if it is used when spoken contributions are needed, so I reframe it as 'tends to do more listening than talking'.

Weaknesses

- *Confrontational*   Because it has negative connotations, I reframe it as 'a preference for facing up to things' because it can actually help when it means the person doesn't let small problems become large, but it can hinder in those situations that genuinely need only time to resolve themselves.

- *Pessimism*   This can help when the person uses it to help people see the potential difficulties but it can hinder when it serves to demoralize people about the problems associated with a project. I tend to reframe it as 'a preference for looking on the negative side of situations'.